PAYMENTS POWER

Increase Your Net Profit 10% or More,
and Improve Cash Flow!

Tom Gerry

More$Faster

A knAct, LLC Publication

knAct, LLC
POB 916301., Longwood, FL 32791

+1(1)407.920.8357

www.paymentspower.com

Payments Power
Increase Your Net Profit 10% or More,
and Improve Cash Flow!

ISBN 978-0-615-30643-8

Library of Congress Control Number: 2009906688
Library of Congress subject headings:
1. Profit Improvement 2. Electronic Payments   3. ACH   4. Credit Cards Payments
5. Debit Card Payments 6. Checks 7. Trade Credit

knAct, LLC books are available at special quantity discounts to use for sales promotions, employee premiums or educational purposes.

This book is dedicated to my wife Diane Gerry. She has encouraged and supported me through all the creation time and effort. David, Adam and Amber, our children, have given me the invaluable support of their interest, critical review and loving belief in my mission.

To Mom and Dad, of that Greatest Generation, my love and admiration and thanks for teaching me the principles of family and life.

It is also dedicated to my nephew John Gerry, who patiently guided and coached me through the labyrinth of our payments world—fragmented, complex and ever-changing.

Contents

More$Faster

www.paymentspower.com

INTRODUCTION

> ## Be a Hero!
>
> Use the **PAYMENTS POWER** framework and tips to reduce your payments costs by one to three percent of revenue.
>
> Take control of your money costs! You deserve the knowledge to understand and manage continually all types of payments coming in and going out – right now and as the payments game changes in the future.
>
> **Increase Your Net Profit 10% or More, and Improve Cash Flow!**
>
> **More$Faster**

Are you looking for fast and smart ways to increase net profit 5% to 20% or more? Are your annual sales between $1 million to $10 billion?

Or, do you provide professional services, such as accounting, or payments technology or processing to businesses or non-profits?

Do you work in a bank or credit union, or for a payments processor and have not been able to answer your customers' questions about their monthly payments processing statements?

If you answered, "Yes", **PAYMENTS POWER** is for you. The simple truth is that profit can be gained from understanding the secrets of payments.

Since the early 70's, I have learned financial services and payments secrets in the United States and on other continents. I built the **PAYMENTS POWER** approach upon a 39 year base of knowledge and action gained as a banker, a consultant and a technology innovator.

I also cofounded a few companies and learned what it means to "make payroll." Like you, I know the real difference between revenue and usable money.

National legislation and anti-trust action is about to make more experimentation possible with your acceptance of different types of payments. You may be able to set minimums and surcharges for more expensive forms of payment. How will you know which payments experiments are producing more profit?

Some experts predict that just as you begin to save money on payments coming in, at almost the same time, your costs of banking, your costs of payments going out will increase, as financial institutions and payments processors react to new regulations. What will be the net effect on your profits of changes in the payments world? What can you do? Will the next payments sales rep who promises you a lower cost for processing really help much? Here are recent results from a business:

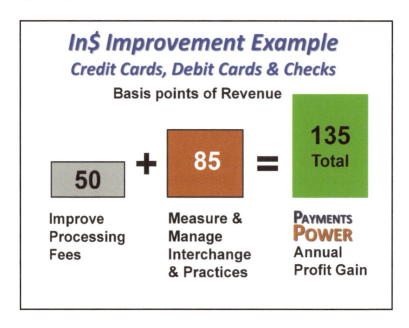

The larger profit improvement came from understanding, measuring and managing payments, on a continuing basis.

Your enterprise might already practice some of the actions I write about, but if you do not have an easy to understand ongoing measurement of your payment systems' performance, some potential profits will remain hidden from you. The purpose of this book is to give you a measurement and management framework and some tips to increase profits from customer payments to you, *In$*; and from payments you make to suppliers and employees, *Out$*.

This is unique-A standard set of performance metrics for all types of payments so you can experiment and measure to improve profits by lowering external and internal payments costs, *How Much*; and to more precisely manage your cash flow, *How Fast*.

Even as the details of interchange pricing, and processing charges and the rules and regulations continue to change the PAYMENTS POWER framework and measurements will work for you.

Recently I bought some two-stroke engine oil at a marine supplies store. I offered an American Express Card® (AMEX) and was told they accepted only Visa® and MasterCard®. The man at the register said they could not afford the 5% fee it would cost them to accept AMEX. I asked how big a purchase might be made with Visa or MasterCard. He said it was common to get paid with credit cards on engine repairs totaling thousands of dollars, but they only lose 1.2% in payment fees.

This illustrates sensitivity to payments costs in a retail setting, but reflects a very superficial understanding and practice.

A real estate broker I met with has two sales offices, a property management company and a title company. They have operating accounts, escrow accounts and commission accounts. They use direct deposit file uploads to their bank to pay property owners the net rents collected, but realtor commissions are still paid with paper checks. The monthly bank account analysis statements **do not** provide a simple way to compare the costs or speed of the checks vs. the electronic ACH direct payments.

It is time to really understand and keep track of all your payments systems costs and delays so you can keep more of your hard earned sales revenue. If you agree, read on and join the **PAYMENTS POWER** movement!

Guy Kawasaki says a short and simple mantra can be more effective than a mission statement. Agreed - I call my approach and framework *MoreMoneyFaster.*

You will see this mantra also as *More$Faster* throughout this book text, figures, tables and diagrams.

Everyone that hears that phrase tells me they are definitely for that idea and want to know how.

Three ways to use this book:

1. Do it Yourself.

2. Use outside consulting to help your team.

3. Sign us up!

The book chapters are summarized so you can go to what interests you without having to read from the beginning to end.

Labels on figures, worksheet examples, and stories are additional guidance to help you find what you want quickly.

Upon hearing the **PAYMENTS POWER** overview, there are three common reactions from decision makers:

1. DIY-"We will do the analysis of our current situation, decide which of the recommended strategies and tactics make sense for us, and then implement ourselves."

2. HELP- "We just do not have the time and resources to do an analysis or to change what will be indicated by the **PAYMENTS POWER** approach. We still want the profit improvement and are willing to pay for outside assistance."

3. JUST DO IT®!- "I know I am wasting money right now. I do not need to do an extensive analysis. Just get me signed up for the best payments solutions right away. We will change whatever we have to for quick and growing profit improvements."

For the Do-It-Yourself organization, study every chapter, download or build your own spreadsheets and deeply understand several months of data for all types of money for each business or location.

For consulting help, just register at www.paymentspower.com and send an e-mail or call. I will work something out to help you with the payments analysis and actions to pursue.

If you are ready to act after just scanning the introduction or chapter summaries that catch your interest, contact me and I will recommend some best of breed options and get you on the path for higher profits from optimized payments systems right away.

Part 1 is about assessing your payments opportunities so you can make informed decisions and set priorities. Chapters 1 through 3 set the stage with self-tests, payments diagrams, and the **PAYMENTS POWER** measurements.

Chapters 4 and 5 will get you started with a straightforward assessment and performance management framework. Chapters 6, 7 and 8 provide tips for identifying payments costs, for both **In$** and **Out$**. Read Chapter 7 if you offer trade credit terms.

Part 2 describes how to increase profits based on opportunities uncovered and prioritized in **Part 1**. **In$** improvements are the topic of Chapter 9, and for those using trade credit see Chapter 10. **Out$** approaches are covered in Chapter 11. Chapters 12 and 13 go into the special aspects of eCommerce and cross border payments.

The final chapter recommends sustaining and continually improving payments performance. After you improve, you may want to know how you are doing compared to other enterprises. There is an opportunity for you to benchmark your results with other **PAYMENTS POWER** participants (each enterprise's data is kept confidential).

The most important insight

Understand your customers' and suppliers' payments behaviors and preferences to harvest a significant portion of your profit improvement. Neither merchant processing statements nor bank account statements alone can reveal those patterns. You will also want to analyze your payments sorted by customer or customer segments over time.

Part 2 will give you some ideas to help spot these customer patterns and experiment to change what matters.

A Note About the Figures

The figures look like presentation slides because many are. You may want to download sets of slides to use for your internal team sessions, for training, and to brainstorm ideas to continually improve your payments systems and increase your profits.

You will find a **PAYMENTS POWER** Summary Action Plan in the Appendix and you can download white papers, forms, more detailed plans, and spreadsheets from the website, www.paymentspower.com .

Change is constant in payments

Because of the Durbin Amendment in 2010 the Federal Reserve will set interchange pricing caps for debit cards in April 2011. I believe this is just the start of many changes in payments costs in the next few years.

Now is the time to begin measuring and managing your costs of payments. As the turmoil plays out, you can improve profits if you know exactly how the changes are affecting your customers and your enterprise.

The details that are referenced in this book are likely to change in the innovative, very competitive payments world. It is impossible to predict exactly what will change or how much.

The **PAYMENTS POWER** framework and metrics are designed to help you recognize the impact on your business and continue to help you improve profits even as the game changes.

FULL DISCLOSURE – In addition to providing consulting services to help improve profits with Payments Power with my company, I work with a national group of independent agents that sell best of breed payments processing services through my nephew's company. The approach is unique – all payments types, all money coming in and going out. Above all, the focus is improving your profit.

PAYMENTS JARGON

Before you even start reading, here are some terms and acronyms you will encounter. The last group are **PAYMENTS POWER** inventions to compress long phrases into abbreviated terms.

ACH and NACHA – The Automated Clearing House is an electronic payment system that has evolved from just direct deposit of payroll and government payments like social security into a robust payments alternative. The National Automated Clearing House Association makes the rules and has guided the evolution.

Basis Points, bps – You are probably very used to thinking about your enterprise in percentage terms. Growth rate, profit margin, market share and many other measures are most often stated as percentages.

Basis points are simply an extension of percentages. Just as 100% is equal to the whole, 100 basis points equals 1%. Basis points are just an easy way to express small or fractional percentages.

If you were describing a stack of currency and coins that totaled $100, then $1 would be 1% of the stack. To describe a quarter as a percentage would be somewhat awkward, perhaps ¼ of 1%. But, out of $100 a quarter is just 25 basis points.

For $1000 the amount of $2.50 is 25 basis points. 25 bps of $10,000 is $25.00. So, if you saved 25 bps of $100 thousand monthly sales, that would be $250 times 12 for a $3 thousand annual profit improvement.

There, now you know. Basis points are easy.

B2C and B2B/G - Business-to-consumer, and business-to–business or business-to-government.

Check 21 - A short way of referring to the national law enacted in the wake of 911 that makes electronic images of the front and back, and the associated data the legal equivalent of an original paper check. Finally, paper checks do not have to be transported to the financial institution holding the accounts they are drawn against.

CNP - Card not present, or customer not present. More costly because more risk of fraudulent use, and more chance of chargeback and exception handling. Some more expensive CNP classifications can be avoided, thereby saving payments costs.

DSO - Days Sales Outstanding is a measure of how long it takes a seller to get paid on trade credit sales. See the **Trade Credit and Factoring** description on a following page in this section.

eCheck - Picture a website shopping cart checkout window displaying an image of a check where you enter your bank's routing and transit number, RT, along with your account number to make an online payment. Or, just as effective, two fields on the screen with an explanation of how to find the RT and bank account number on the magnetic ink line on the bottom of your check. Or, by telephone, you might say or key in these two numbers which are used to create and process an ACH payment, a withdrawal from your account, without the need for creating a paper check at all.

ePay or ePayment – A simple way to classify a payment type as **ePay** is by elimination. If the payment is not by currency and coin, not by paper check or money order or travelers check, nor by a debit or credit card, then the original payment is likely **ePay**. This would usually include wire transfers and originated ACH deposits and withdrawals. The original form is important to classify because profit improvement may be found in somehow changing or improving that original payment type.

Gateway - A website or application interfaced payment authorization and capture service, which may offer additional fraud prevention and chargeback resolution features. More than just a standalone terminal online interface, some gateways may be used to make a PC into a virtual terminal with attached card reader, signature pad and PIN pad.

Payments gateways often are integrated with the business software such as restaurant or veterinary applications.

Level 2 & Level 3 Data - Business purchase detail information that, if transmitted along with the normal information, can substantially reduce payments costs on purchasing cards, and various other business card transactions.

Payment Processing, Network Costs and Interchange – Payments costs for the electronic and paper information and money routing and control can be roughly divided into three components:
1) payment processing, the services provided to the seller/merchant,
2) payments network infrastructure and settlement costs,
3) interchange paid to the financial institution for marketing, setup, transaction processing, posting and maintenance of the buyer/card holder's credit or deposit account.

The seller sends transactions to and gets usable money and statements from payments processors and financial institutions.

The buyer chooses from many forms of payments to tender to a seller and gets statements showing the decreases in usable money in bank deposit accounts or decreases in available balances for charging with credit card accounts, or Trade Credit aged balances (see Trade Credit and Factoring below).

The payments acquiring, clearing and issuing players price and collect for their services in many different ways. Much of the payments clearing and settlement costs, even on the buyers' side, are paid by the seller. You may find hidden profits in different steps and in different payments types shown in Payments Chain diagrams used throughout this book to illustrate the many steps from a sale to final changes in buyer's and seller's usable account balances.

P Cards – Purchasing cards are an innovation in payments for businesses that streamline and reduce overhead in some B2B transactions; used instead of trade credit typically for budgeted departmental purchases. **P Cards** eliminate the delays and relatively high costs of purchase order processes for smaller transactions. **P Cards** are not used for larger supply chain purchases that require a more complex purchasing approval, negotiation and control process. Payment is more flexible, and Trade credit is effectively interest free borrowing of working funds.

Trade Credit and Factoring – The most important primary payment type in B2B/G, but also used in B2C for large purchases. **Trade Credit** is simply the seller providing goods or services to buyers in exchange for a formal promise to pay in usable money sometime in the future, perhaps with a down payment to start. In effect, the seller makes a short term loan to the buyer. **Factoring** is the seller getting usable money much faster than the seller expects to get it from the buyer by selling accounts receivables to a third party. There are many variations, costs and risk levels of this practice.

Upcharges, Downgrades or Surcharges – The reclassification of card transactions resulting in higher payments costs due to various operational reasons such as neglecting to batch out by the daily cut-off time, or not including data like address verification.

PAYMENTS POWER diagrams, measurements and abbreviations:

Payments Chains – Diagrams used to visualize the flows of information and processing that result in sellers receiving usable money from buyers of goods and services. Useful for identifying value-add steps which generate payments costs, and consume time.

In$ – The amount of any and all types of payments received by sellers from buyers. Money you receive from sales, excluding sales taxes.

Out$ – The amount of any and all types of payments made by buyers to sellers. Money you pay out.

M$, L$ - Simple dashboard measurements that compare the money value performance all types of payments, ***M$*** for receipts, ***In$,*** and ***L$*** for disbursements, ***Out$***.

M$*** for ***In$, the remaining amount of usable money per $100 in sales after subtracting all the payments costs a seller incurs. Your profit improvement comes as you increase this measure to get closer to $100. **More** money, a bigger ***M$*** is better for ***In$.***

L$*** for ***Out$, the amount of usable money consumed per $100 of purchases paid after adding all payments costs a buyer incurs. This will be more than $100, reduce this to improve profit. **Less** is better

F$* - Simple dashboard measurements of the speed dimension of payments performance. *F$ allows comparison of the processing and clearing time of all types of payments.

F$* for *In$, the number of business days from the day a buyer tenders a payment for goods or services received until the seller, your enterprise, has that payment as usable money in your bank account available balance.

F$* for *Out$, the number of business days from when the buyer, your enterprise, tenders payment for goods or services and when the usable money, the available balance, in your bank account is reduced by the payment.

More$Faster

www.paymentspower.com

PART 1

Take the Gloves Off - Assess And Decide

To uncover and harvest profits hidden in your payments system requires measurement and insight and judgment. **Part 1** can help you focus on the most profitable improvements and then see how you are doing month by month. First, you have to determine *What to change*, and then in **Part 2** you will find ideas and guidance on *How to change*.

This is a performance improvement approach, not an accounting exercise. So, be sure not to try to measure every possible payments cost noted in this section in your first round of payments improvements. The 80/20 rule will serve you well.

After you pick the low hanging fruit in the first round, come back in a future improvements cycle to **Part 1** and consider other costs that may then be the most valuable candidates for improvement.

More$Faster

www.paymentspower.com

1 TEST YOURSELF

In this chapter you will find two quick tests that will indicate if you can improve your profits using **PAYMENTS POWER** measurements, tools and tips:

1. For payments you receive - *In$*

2. For payments you send – *Out$*

An overview of payments trends is included with more detail at www.paymentspower.com so you can be aware of changes in the marketplace.

You will learn about two innovations that make these profit improvements possible now:

1. Self-service electronic transactions origination

2. Complete transparency in credit and debit card processing

The chapter includes a story about a misleading merchant services sales practice you may find familiar.

1 TEST YOURSELF

A recent local *Business Journal Small Business Survival Guide* caught my eye. The business experts all advised the reader to be ruthless on costs, but do "smart" cuts; not "easy" cuts that can cripple your future. In my 37 year career I have been deeply involved with knowledge-based ways to improve profits without resorting to the "easy" cuts of layoffs and reduced marketing the experts warned against.

I have created **PAYMENTS POWER** to provide a set of knowledge-based profit improvement tools. It is a "how to" for field use. As a business owner who has started three companies and has also worked for larger enterprises, and been through mergers and downsizing, I am very passionate about this topic.

There is certainly a power imbalance in the marketplace. Can you negotiate with Visa, MasterCard, PayPal™, American Express, the Federal Reserve System (FED), or international banks? Call me if you can - I want to know you.

> According to Cyber-Source, in the Internet world profit improvements of 5-8% of revenue are possible through active management of ePayments - How?
>
> Through cost savings combined with higher sales conversions.

I believe superior knowledge and execution can help you overcome the payments systems power imbalance. The profits you are losing today in excess payments cost and delays in usable money are just as important a waste as any process inefficiency in a manufacturing line or in a back office workflow.

In 2010 the United States passed a financial reform act which includes changes relating to payments costs, especially debit card interchange. However, even if the regulations give enterprises mandated relief from some payments costs, there will still be profit opportunities to uncover by better understanding and managing your payments systems. Some experts believe the door is opening for more experimentation with payments policies and practices to reduce costs.

Working with a company recently, we found that with a well-known debit and credit card processor they were only realizing $97.23

out of every $100 in credit card sales and only $98.33 of every $100 in debit card revenue.

After the **PAYMENTS POWER** analysis we helped them increase these usable funds to $98.44 and $98.77, respectively. This resulted in a net profit improvement of 11.2%.

Next, the company planned further profit improvement by using web-based ACH originated payments to their major suppliers instead of paper checks.

Why should you care?

- Payments improvements go straight to bottom line profit, with little or no capital investment, and many can happen quickly.

- Payments improvements may increase sales by adding choices for customers.

Before you go any further, here are two rules of thumb to quickly assess whether you should care about this approach.

Measure Usable In$

Do you know how much of your sales money actually ends up in your bank account, and how fast it gets there after the sale is completed? What matters is the money in your bank account, not just your sales revenue. So, what makes these amounts different? **Your payments systems costs and delays!**

Here is an easy test to see if you should care:

1. Pick a period; last month, last three months or last year.

2. Make a quick estimate of all your costs for *In$*, including processing and interchange on cards, losses on checks that bounce, all bank charges, even counting and wrapping currency and coin you receive.

3. Divide the payments costs by your total sales, *In$*, for the same period. This gives you a percentage of sales.

4. Multiply by 100 to convert the percentage back to dollars.

5. Subtract from $100.

6. This is your **M$** for **In$,** the remaining usable money from every $100 in sales after payments costs are subtracted.

7. If this is $98 or less you are likely to find value in the PAYMENTS POWER information and approach.

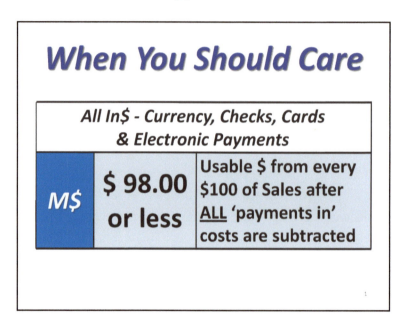

Assess the delay of In$

A recent U.S. Postal Service survey of business owners asked what the impact would be of the proposed elimination of one day of mail delivery, either on Tuesday or Saturday. A majority, 52%, of the people surveyed said their business would be hurt by the change. The most negative impact cited is the loss of a day on check deposits; the interest lost, but most importantly the delay in usable funds.

This book may help reduce the negative impact by changing mailed checks to electronic payments. However, you will find trade-offs between faster payments, **F$**, and reduced processing costs to increase usable money, **M$**. For example, with ACH processors you can find many alternatives in combinations of speed in gaining usable money and ACH payments costs. For example, one processor will send same day deposits on telephone check payments submitted by 10:00 am, but the payments cost is nearly 3% of the revenue amount.

A much lower cost alternative improves **M$** but increases **F$**. You might replace a telephone credit card transaction that costs about 3% and is in your bank account two business days later, with an ACH transaction that costs less than 1% but is not available until four business days later, twice as long.

Trade Credit - Days Sales Outstanding

The accounting measure of Days Sales Outstanding (DSO) is used in enterprises to assess efficiency of collecting accounts receivable balances, trade credit extended to buyers. DSO is a good tool calculated on the internal accounting system, but does not include the timing gap between the internal accounting bank account balance and the available balance at your financial institution.

Banks call this *float*, or *unavailable funds*, and use it to reduce your available and usable balances for one, two or more days.

That gap can and should be measured in addition to DSO and can be squeezed to improve cash flow and increase profits. We will also explore recent trade credit factoring innovations that can dramatically improve accounts receivable DSO even as you extend longer trade credit terms to your customers. Seems impossible, but I'll explain later in the book.

For those readers who are implementing "Lean" and practicing continual improvement, this book is about eliminating waste in payments processes. In the 2008 analysis of the *Supply Chain Top 25* by AMR Research, significant progress was noted in industry leaders' *cash to cash* metrics.

Cash to cash is inventory days plus payables outstanding days minus receivables outstanding days. In supply chain terms, **PAYMENTS POWER** supports improvements in the *cash to cash* performance framework. By increasing usable money from **In$** and reducing costs of **Out$**, and focusing on delays in payments, **PAYMENTS POWER** directly impacts both quantity and speed components of the *cash to cash* supply chain metrics.

Out$

Although accounts payable costs may be more difficult to estimate, around the world there are documented cases of reengineered back office processes that improved over 50% in cost and speed. **PAYMENTS POWER** can help you focus on all *Out$* costs, including internal costs such as wasted time and external costs like the money you pay for preprinted business checks.

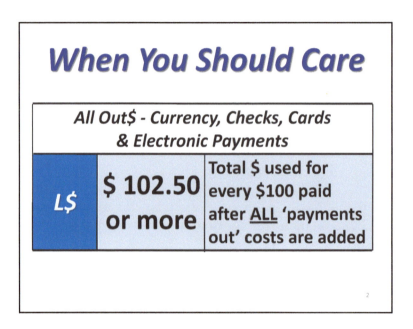

Here is the quick test:

1. Pick a period; last month, last three months or last year.

2. Make a quick estimate of all your *Out$* costs, including supplies and mailing/delivery, bank charges, and the internal accounts payable costs.

3. Divide the payments costs by your total A/P disbursements for the same period. This gives you cost as a percentage of *Out$.*

4. Multiply by 100 to convert this percentage back to dollars.

5. Add to $100.

6. This is your *L$* for *Out$,* the total money used to pay each $100 of bills after adding the payments costs.

7. If this is $102.50 or more, you are likely to find value in the **PAYMENTS POWER** information and approach.

If you are still paying suppliers or employees by paper check, the total of all your **Out$** costs may even exceed $10 per written check.

The average amount of your checks will determine your total dollars used per $100. If you disburse larger checks, your payments costs per $100 will be lower.

Even if your total amount of money used is lower than the rule of thumb of $102.50, you may want to gain another benefit—faster, more precise and predictable cash flow.

Overview of Payments Trends

Payments are a very complex and fast changing aspect of our world. An example of the complexity just from the credit card type is the nearly 400 page Visa *U.S. Interchange Reimbursement Rate Qualification Guide*. Do you accept Visa? Have you read this document and does it help you improve your profits? Probably not.

Payments have been evolving since the beginning of the human race. Barter in goods and services, cattle, cowry shells, leather money, silver and gold, private promissory notes, paper money backed by gold, paper and electronic promises of trusted institutions backed by government sponsored deposit insurance, travelers checks and money orders and gift cards are all variations of money. Some are more useful than others, some more liquid, and some are more costly for enterprises.

There is a marketing campaign, a war, being waged by the card issuers and associations against other forms of payments. As individuals you and I receive credit card solicitations almost daily. For instance, by signing up for the Investment Rewards American Express Card, 2% of every purchase would be deposited in my investment account.

While there may be alternative perspectives of the credit card rewards programs, here is one way to view them:

In this specific example American Express is taking 2% of the merchant's gross revenue when I make a purchase to buy my loyalty for Amex, not for the merchant. It seems that most rewards programs are paid for by the selling businesses but the merchants do not get the primary loyalty benefit. Perhaps this means the "interchange" is too high by 2%, or with a closed loop payments model like Amex, at least 2% of the fees collected by Amex from the business are not really needed to process payments and yield profit, but are being used to buy market share from other payments alternatives that may be substantially less costly for merchants.

To really understand money and payments, you might consider an analogy. "The medium is the message" is a concept that proposes that various media, such as books, movies and television, dramatically affect how people experience and receive information or entertainment content.

Interestingly, with payments, the medium becomes the content, the money. But the most useful form of money resides in the end result of payments—a change in balance in the enterprise's account maintained at a trusted financial institution; funds available to pay bills, make payroll, purchase equipment and materials, and reward owners. Likewise, the various payment media, even though containing the same monetary amount being conveyed, can deliver value faster or slower, with greater or lesser risk, and at higher and lower external and internal costs, with different customer experiences.

Find out how the recent transparency in credit card transaction pricing and rules can help you discover and keep more money.

To find profits hidden in payments, it is worth looking at payment trends and some significant events.

Debit card transactions grew the fastest since 2000. In 2009 about half of the withdrawals from deposit accounts were originated with check cards, not counting ATM cash or prepaid card transactions. Checks were down to only 30%. PIN based withdrawals were only about one fourth the number of signature debit card transactions. Check cards transaction amounts averaged about $40.

ACH payments grew 20% recently. With flat growth in credit card payments and an absolute decline in check volumes ACH transactions filled the gap. Some experts, however, say that over 45% of consumer spending, and 85% of small and medium business spending in the U.S. is still in the form of cash or checks. In the 2009 and 2010 recession economy payments growth of all types changed dramatically. Some research shows credit card transactions stalled, with a shift, at least temporarily, more to debit cards, electronic payments and even back to checks and cash. However, other reports say credit card debt is at an all time high.

Large retailer lawsuit against the credit card associations —Several legal actions culminated in a class action anti-trust lawsuit in 2003 led by Walmart® and other large retailers against Visa and MasterCard. The class included 7 million businesses and the three major retail federations. The multi-billion-dollar settlement and the elimination of the "honor all cards" rule was a victory for retailers.

A good consequence of the power struggle, the pressure from businesses, is that the interchange rules, costs and structure are now much more transparent. They are still very complicated, and few in business understand all the layers and elements of card payments processing costs.

Many people I have interviewed feel that in the years following the huge settlement, even as some interchange rates were reduced, unfortunately Visa and MasterCard have slowly but surely dramatically raised average card transaction costs.

National legislation—The Durbin amendment introduced mid-year 2010 in the financial reform effort reflects the revolt by sellers against the continuing rise in payments costs. Whatever the legal and regulatory details specify, more freedom is emerging in minimums and incentives to get buyers to use lower cost payment types.

Merchants Payments Coalition—This group of merchants is carrying on the fight to even out the power imbalance, primarily through lobbying for legislation. You may have noticed some signs in stores asking for petition signatures to support their efforts.

Emergence of person–to-person electronic payments—Started by PayPal for online auctions like eBay®. In the early years it was attractive due to worries about putting account numbers out on the Internet and having hackers run up unauthorized purchases. Today, beyond their original mission and after being purchased by eBay, PayPal and similar Internet-based competitors have expanded their scope dramatically. And if you do not understand your eCommerce alternatives, your current processor may be eating into your profits beyond the value you receive in using their payments solutions.

Much stronger Internet security - Multi-factor and terminal authentication can now be implemented with web-based payment technology for transaction integrity. Tokenization is emerging to protect card and account numbers in mobile and online payments.

Zero interchange credit cards – New innovations are surfacing. This represents a very promising value for merchants and businesses. However, one zero interchange card company appears to be struggling to grow the number of cardholders. (Interchange does reward issuers.)

Mobile payments - Smartphone based, another convenience for shoppers, but maybe another layer of cost you will have to bear, or at least measure and manage. However, if you collect payments in the field, like pizza delivery or plumbing repair, why not swipe a card and capture a signature on your employee's smart phone for a lower cost card present transaction?

True factoring for small and medium businesses - An affordable way to achieve the paradox of accelerating the accounts receivable conversion into usable money while offering longer trade credit terms to business customers for a dramatic competitive advantage.

Department of Justice actions – Three largest US card associations have been sued for anti-competitive practices. All the settlement details are not known at the time of publication, but the message is clear – the associations are losing the power to prevent businesses from improving their payments costs. Timing is right for this book!

Payments Innovations and Advances

Recent advances make the **PAYMENTS POWER** approach now possible with your own payment systems:

1. **Self-service Automated Clearing House (ACH) transaction origination and risk management.** This advance is enabled by the web and comes with heavy duty multi-factor security. You may find these capabilities in business online banking, and other bank cash management services, or from independent ACH processors.

2. **More transparent credit and debit card payments processing and settlement.** Transactions are identified with the association standard classification descriptions, and processing fees are explicit and fixed, not hidden and variable. Also, statement information is available online and easier to understand with built-in performance improvement measures.

ACH, an electronic funds transfer, is a mature, and efficient electronic payments method few people are aware of, but most are affected by. The new web-based self-service approaches are convenient and secure. The classic ACH capabilities continue, but now there are add-on *turbochargers*, I describe as *ACH 2.0*. I will explain this with examples throughout the book. In 2011 mobile ACH payments, including text based from mobile phones, are likely to be supported by expanded NAHCA rules.

For readers that want more details of payments trends studies and statistics, go to the website, www.paymentspower.com , for free white papers, or to review the Blog. You do not need to read these to improve profits from payments, but some readers may find the information interesting.

Before we go on though, a warning.

There are many payment proposals presented that are misleading, perhaps deceptive, and certainly not transparent.

There is a growing sense of frustration, even anger, in the people using payments processing services. Certainly this is due to rising costs. But just as aggravating are the sales practices and the monthly statements that are nearly impossible to understand and audit.

There are many payments processors, independent sales organizations, and individual payments sales professionals that believe in and practice the best business approach – they want to help you succeed with their payments services and be more profitable, while at the same time their business grows and is also profitable.

Unfortunately, there are many payments industry players that act in ways not to your advantage. You have to have the knowledge of the game to deal effectively with them. Here is an example:

Deception Story

Andy, the owner of a fine dining restaurant, received a merchant services payments processing proposal worksheet that claimed he could save $75 per month on Visa/MasterCard/Discover card receipts of $23,000 and American Express card transactions of $8,000.

The competitor proposed lowering the authorization fee per item from $0.10 to $0.03 (savings of $22 on 311 transactions). They also told Andy they would eliminate any monthly fixed fees (another $24 in savings).

But, on another worksheet line the payments processor proposed to raise the discount rate processing margin from 0.15% to 0.30%, a 15 basis point increase. (On $23,000 in sales an increase of about $34 monthly) The last change proposed was to lower the pass-through processing fee on Amex transactions from $0.20 to $0.05. However, there were 82 Amex transactions that month so 15 cents saved on the actual number of Amex tickets would just be about $12. Therefore, the total net monthly savings would be merely $24, not $75 as claimed.

The proposal monthly savings was overstated by $50! Was this just sloppy work or deliberate misrepresentation? You decide.

Take the power into your hands

Consider a similar business advance in self-service. LegalZoom™ was created by lawyers for people to use for self-service legal documents. Like LegalZoom, **PAYMENTS POWER** was designed for self-service payments systems optimization. Web-based self-service ACH, similar to LegalZoom, puts power in your hands. Also, just as LegalZoom does not eliminate the need for professional legal advice, readers of **PAYMENTS POWER** should supplement self-service with the best professional payments processing and services they can find.

Payments systems improvements are "smart cuts"—no layoffs, no reduction in marketing—just direct bottom line profit improvement. And, by reducing paper, **PAYMENTS POWER** is "green" in more than one way.

PAYMENTS POWER is a direct and simple approach to arm you with knowledge to overcome misinformation and to understand and manage the complexity of payments systems. The mantra of *More$Faster* resonates with most people because we all know more profits, more revenue and lower costs are good. And life is better with more usable money sooner than later.

Take Action

1. Make a quick estimate of your payments received costs per $100 of sales, subtract and see if the remainder is less than $98, if yes, PAYMENTS POWER may be for you.

2. Estimate payments costs per $100 paid out, add to the $100 paid, and if the total is more than $102.50, PAYMENTS POWER may be for you.

3. Find out how long it takes for payments from sales to become usable money in your bank account. If longer than two days, PAYMENTS POWER may be for you.

4. Determine how long from when you pay before you lose the use of that money in your bank account. If more than two to four days, or the time varies unpredictably more than two days longer or shorter, then PAYMENTS POWER may be for you.

If you are curious, look at alternatives, but if the math does not make sense, be skeptical. Get an objective analysis, or read this book and figure it out.

More$Faster

www.paymentspower.com

2 PAYMENTS CHAINS

In this chapter you will see the building blocks of payments revealed.

First I will explain a simple diagram for understanding most payments processes. I call it a Payment Chain.

A story of paper checks payments is told to show how the payment chain diagram is used.

Next you will see a "behind the curtain" payment diagram that reveals much more of the complexity of payments.

A software integration story will illustrate one of the profit reduction dilemmas you may face in choosing payments solutions.

Finally I will share my opinion about the payments help you should seek.

2 PAYMENTS CHAINS

I will use payments chain diagrams throughout the book to illustrate all the points where your sales revenue incurs payments costs on the way to becoming usable money, and where you generate costs paying others.

You will see a simple diagram and a more detailed "behind the curtain" version used to map the steps of processing various payment types. For example, you will see where a PIN check card transaction differs from signature debit, and several variations of check payment chains, each with different payments costs and speed.

The process step diagram shows the paths payments follow to move the money from the buyer's deposit or credit account to the seller's deposit account. While some buyers do not have formal deposit accounts, but operate just with cash or near cash such as money orders or stored value cards, the diagrams will still serve their purpose. Just think of that personal "stash" of near cash as the buyer's deposit account.

Let's walk through the simple payments chain diagram sections and components on the following page. You can use it as a tool to help understand payments from the perspective of a seller and as a buyer relative to your suppliers' payments chains.

Buy Column

The start of the transaction and money flow of the payments chain is the **Tender**, shown in the left hand column of the diagram. Most people are familiar with all these kinds of tender except trade credit.

Trade credit is an initial **Tender** in business-to-business, B2B, where it is common to order and receive goods and services well in advance of obtaining an invoice and making a payment eventually with another type of tender, most often a business check.

If the payment is eventually made with a business check, why consider the trade credit a kind of tender? Because a trade credit is a business credit account, a short term loan restricted to only buying goods and services from the company taking the credit risk. The purchase

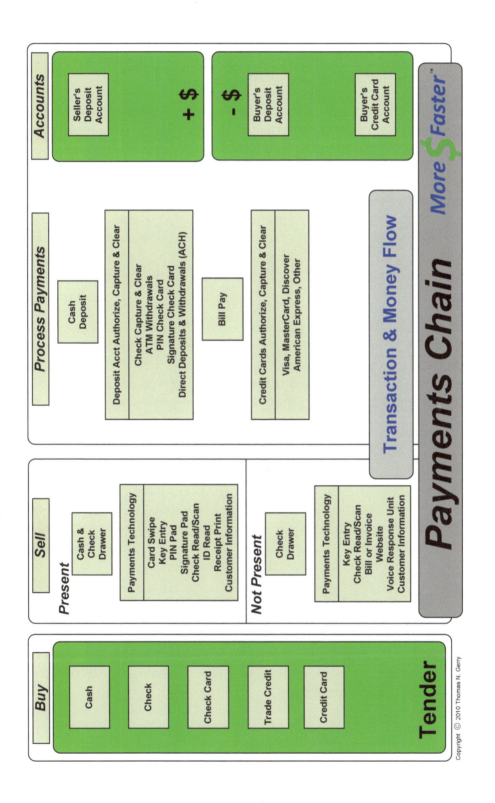

Payments Chain

Transaction & Money Flow

More $ Faster™

Tender

Accounts

Seller's Deposit Account

+ $

− $

Buyer's Deposit Account

Buyer's Credit Card Account

Process Payments

Cash Deposit

Deposit Acct Authorize, Capture & Clear

Check Capture & Clear
ATM Withdrawals
PIN Check Card
Signature Check Card
Direct Deposits & Withdrawals (ACH)

Bill Pay

Credit Cards Authorize, Capture & Clear

Visa, MasterCard, Discover
American Express, Other

Sell

Present

Cash & Check Drawer

Payments Technology

Card Swipe
Key Entry
PIN Pad
Signature Pad
Check Read/Scan
ID Read
Receipt Print
Customer Information

Not Present

Check Drawer

Payments Technology

Key Entry
Check Read/Scan
Bill or Invoice
Website
Voice Response Unit
Customer Information

Buy

Cash

Check

Check Card

Trade Credit

Credit Card

19

order or notification to ship under a negotiated supply agreement, accepted under trade credit, has the same buying effect as cash, checks or credit cards. As a business buyer you tender the purchase order and get the products and services in exchange.

At its heart trade credit is much the same as a branded credit card account, except the buyer controls when the short term loan repayment is made, and is not presented with a monthly credit card statement containing a rigid due date.

Eventually the business pays the invoice with some other form of payment, which is analogous to someone making a payment in response to a credit card statement, it only seems like paying the invoice is buying the goods. The reality is that the credit underwriting decision and business relationship makes trade credit real tender used to buy the goods and services.

Some businesses sell their accounts receivables to a **Factor**, in effect exchanging the buyer's tender, the trade credit, to receive useful money faster in their deposit account well in advance of receiving payment from an invoice. The money from the invoice repays the **Factor** and is actually a different transaction than the original purchase, even though closely related.

Even consumers practice this method for buying some things. For example, we replaced our air conditioning system at home recently. We signed a contract, a one-time purchase order and gave a deposit. Days later the components and the installation crew arrived. Only after everything was running did we pay the balance due. Two types of tender were used, a purchase contract, (which was a promise to pay), and checks - a deposit check, and the completion check.

Why bother understanding this? Because there are costs, delays and risks, which the buyer or seller, or both, bear in the use of trade credit tender. A cost not seen by the buyer but very obvious to a seller, is the discount or interest and fees a **Factor** charges for buying accounts receivables. This can be a significant percentage of revenue, and therefore an even bigger percentage of profit.

If you are a purchase order buyer you may benefit from understanding your seller's expenses paid to **Factors** to accelerate their cash flow. If you can pay faster, you might negotiate a significant purchase discount.

Sell Column

The second column from the left edge of the diagram includes seller payments tools and tasks.

Because payments costs can be so much higher when the transaction is not face to face, the payments chain diagram separates the *present* and *not-present* transactions. Although there are payments building blocks common to both, you will notice the differences.

For example, PIN pads and signature pads are useful face to face, but a PIN payment may be much more profitable than a signature debit transaction commonly described as 'Credit' or 'Offline'.

Buyers and sellers that are not face to face can use telephones, Internet websites, mailed bills and invoices and voice response units.

Many companies find profit improvement opportunity first in the transactions that are classified as CNP, *Customer not present, or Card not present*.

Process Payments Column

Cash deposits are diagrammed separately because they deserve consideration of their special costs and risks if currency and coin is a significant portion of revenue.

Note that the *Deposit Accounts Authorize, Capture & Clear* box breaks out five types of processing to draw attention to very different payments cost due to different processing requirements.

Bill payment, both personal and business, is a separate box also because of different steps and costs that may deserve study for uncovering profit, and accelerating cash flow.

The *Credit Cards Authorize, Capture & Clear* box includes very complex layers of pricing and transaction classifications that can significantly affect your overall payments processing and settlement costs.

For many this will be a starting point to look for hidden profit opportunities.

Accounts

These boxes represent the most usable money belonging to the buyers and sellers. While currency and coin may seem the most liquid kind of money, collected funds in checking accounts can make payroll, purchase raw materials as well as other goods and services, pay dividends to investors, and pay taxes.

The ultimate purpose of the payments chain transactions is to move money from the buyers' accounts to the sellers' accounts. Here is a story and a payments chain diagram example to illustrate how to visualize the costs, delays and risks in those process steps that accomplish the money movement.

Paper Checks Story

James, the head of store operations, does not want any of his staff wasting time trying to collect bounced checks.

So, like many businesses that take checks, he contracted for a check guarantee service. Every check received at the counter is scanned in a terminal along with the driver's license. The information is validated online and the check is denied or approved. Some of the checks are converted to ACH transactions, but more than half are not.

Except for a stop payment, they have not had a returned check all of last year. Was this due to the guarantee, or just the type of customer writing the checks? More on this story later.

The check guarantee and ACH conversion cost has been about 1.6% of check revenue. Check guarantee for every check was more expensive than PIN debit—as much as 50 basis points. The guarantee is paid on *every* check received, a kind of insurance, but nationally only 0.5% of checks written are returned for insufficient funds.

Some of the operational objectives are met with the check guarantee service, but is it possible to prevent taking fraudulent or insufficient checks at a lower cost?

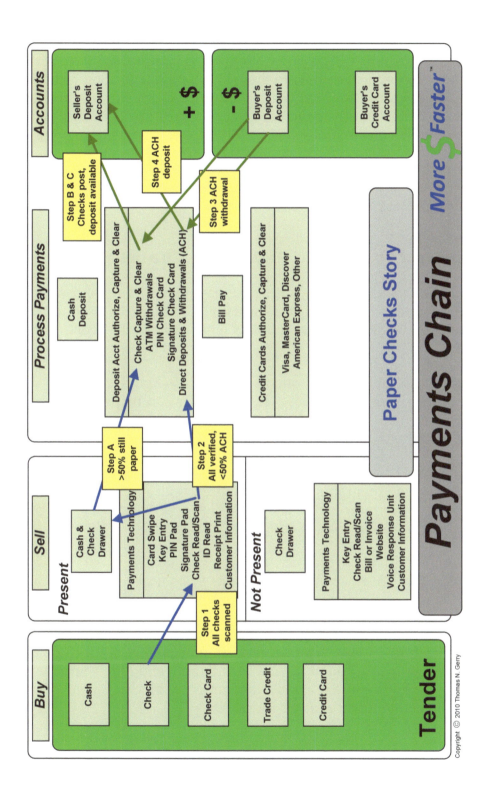

Payments Chain

More $ Faster™

Paper Checks Story

Buy — Tender

- Cash
- Check
- Check Card
- Trade Credit
- Credit Card

Sell

Present

- Cash & Check Drawer
- Payments Technology
  - Card Swipe
  - Key Entry
  - PIN Pad
  - Signature Pad
  - Check Read/Scan
  - ID Read
  - Receipt Print
  - Customer Information

Not Present

- Check Drawer
- Payments Technology
  - Key Entry
  - Check Read/Scan
  - Bill or Invoice
  - Website
  - Voice Response Unit
  - Customer Information

Process Payments

- Cash Deposit
- Deposit Acct Authorize, Capture & Clear
  - Check Capture & Clear
  - ATM Withdrawals
  - PIN Check Card
  - Signature Check Card
  - Direct Deposits & Withdrawals (ACH)
- Bill Pay
- Credit Cards Authorize, Capture & Clear
  - Visa, MasterCard, Discover
  - American Express, Other

Accounts

- Seller's Deposit Account + $
- Buyer's Deposit Account − $
- Buyer's Credit Card Account

Step 1 — All checks scanned

Step A — >50% still paper

Step 2 — All verified, <50% ACH

Step 3 ACH withdrawal

Step 4 ACH deposit

Step B & C — Checks post, deposit available

23

Let's consider the story about paper checks and reflect on how the payments chain diagrams was used. Follow the flow shown in the payments chain diagram of this story. Notice the complexity, the operational steps needed just to handle these check payments. Some checks are handled electronically after the initial scan, but others are deposited in paper check form at the bank because they were business checks ineligible for ACH conversion.

This diagram of the story is a good example of how you can use the payments chain to visually document a current situation and then brainstorm process improvements.

Behind the Curtain Payments Chains

The *Behind the Curtain* version of the payments chain seems much more complicated, but can help you assess all the elements of your payments costs and delays for ***In$*** and ***Out$*** when you want a deeper analysis.

Notice the additional components that come to light from *Behind the Curtain* in the paper checks story. The diagrams can help you identify profit improvement opportunities on a continual basis, and provide a training tool for your team.

In Chapter 11 you will find both the simple payments chain and the *Behind the Curtain* diagrams further enhanced with PayPal capabilities primarily for eCommerce. That chapter will also reveal current and potential use of PayPal in "brick and mortar" situations.

The *Behind the Curtain* diagram on the next page also illustrates why you should find an independent payments system expert that can assemble the best combination of capabilities, the best of breed, for each business model you operate.

In contrast, many merchant service companies may not include all the types of payments you need, and may bundle and hide component costs, thus perhaps concealing and inadvertently blocking your profit identification and improvement opportunities.

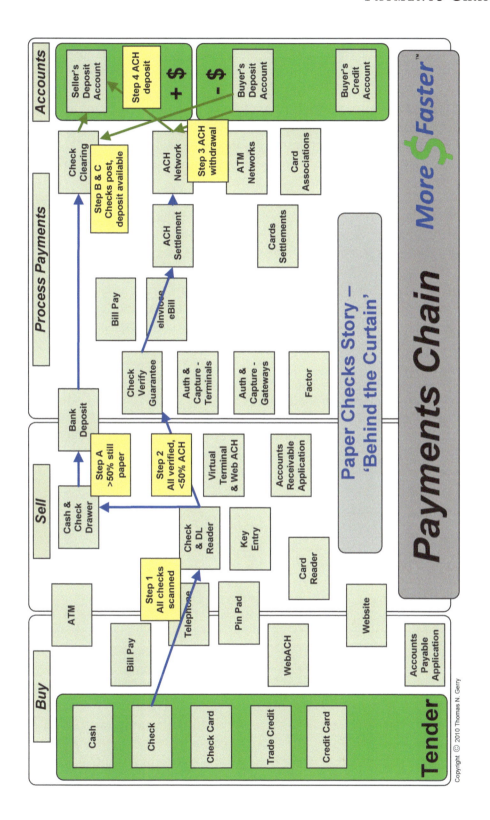

"Good News, Bad News" Story

Dr. John's veterinary clinic runs like a well-oiled machine. The pets and their owners really love the staff and the services provided. Part of the efficiency is due to the integrated card payments capability within the veterinary application software.

When a pet owner is ready to pay, the vet software calculates the amount due and if the payment is by card, a window opens, the card is swiped through a wedge reader attached to the PC, and either the customer enters a number through an attached PIN pad or signs a signature pad. This process is slightly faster than using a separate card terminal, and eliminates the possibility of errors due to entering the same information twice.

So far, so good. The integration brings efficiency, but does it support effective payments management?—When the monthly card processing statement arrives, the frustration begins. The statement information presentation and calculations are based on a surcharge approach. The processing fee is first calculated on 100% of the various types of non-PIN transactions at the *qualified* discount and item rate (1.775% and 11 cents for Visa). But, only 8% of the transactions are actually *qualified*. Later in the statement, presented in an entirely different format, *mid-qualified* and *non-qualified* surcharge fees are calculated and identified with vague descriptions.

The statements hide the information Dr. John needs to improve profits. Is this on purpose?

Caveat Emptor! Be careful to understand the payments costs and information quality of integrated point of sale or backroom accounting software applications. My entire career I have worked to apply and integrate technologies to improve people's productivity and prevent errors, so this advice goes against my grain. Unfortunately, applications software suppliers have often chosen to offer integrated and bundled payments processing that is more costly and less transparent, the worst of the traditional merchant services world.

You should consider the trade-off. Is the seamless point of sale integration worth lower profit? Here are some questions to consider if you are using or considering using payments processing integrated in your applications software:

1. Are you able to see every month the exact payments classification and costs, including interchange, authorization and settlement fees and processing costs?

2. Does your software supplier share in the processing revenue? Is this disclosed?

3. Does the payments integration include lower cost alternatives to cards such as eChecks and recurring ACH?

4. Does the integration include all the data needed to qualify transactions for the lowest payments costs?

Based on the answers to these questions, ask if the keystrokes saved are worth forgoing the chance to improve profit by ½% to maybe 1 ½% (50 to 100 bps) of your revenue. For $2 million in sales that could be up to $30 thousand annually. Standalone terminals or PC based virtual terminals may be a higher profit choice than using payments integrated with an application, with more flexibility to change payment processors if you wish.

Independent Payments Help

Do you buy tires directly from a Goodyear® factory salesperson after also talking with the Michelin® factory? Most likely not. Many people research tire prices and availability at local tire stores that carry several brands and also rely on word of mouth recommendations from friends and family. The same applies to other products.

How do you choose payments processing? Most businesspeople are experts in their respective field, but not in payments. Unfortunately, the payments world is very fragmented and changing fast, so even if you wanted to, it would be very difficult to find and keep track of the best combination of payment suppliers.

There are over 700 companies in the *Visa Global List of Payment Card Industry Data Security Standard Validated Service Providers* and nearly 440 entries in the *Visa List of PABP Validated Payment Applications*. That is just the Visa universe. Do you have the time to research all payment solutions and keep track of their relative value as the payments world keeps changing? Probably not.

Many business people and nonprofit managers simply buy all payment processing from their primary financial institution. This is the simple approach. The **PAYMENTS POWER** framework and measurements will let you know exactly what that approach costs. Have you ever asked your banker to explain your merchant services monthly statement? Some bankers will be able to and some will not.

So, what are your options? If you buy payments processing just from you primary financial institution, or based on the lowest quoted processing price you may be leaving significant profits on the table.

Of course, there are highly knowledgeable captive agents representing processors that truly sell with a 'win-win' philosophy. They succeed by representing your best interests. Hang on to that relationship if you have it. Still, I recommend finding an independent agent organization, not just for credit cards but for all types of payments systems, for processing your money in, ***In$,*** and money out, ***Out$***.

Different companies, and even distinct lines of business within an enterprise, can require very different templates to improve, switch or add payments components for more profit, to lower costs and increase sales. Single company agents are unlikely to help you with the three strategies since some of the best actions for you may go against the goals of their employer.

In addition to any great existing payments relationship, look for an independent payments orchestrator, an agent that will configure the best combination of payments building blocks to underwrite, host, acquire, authorize, capture, settle and service all your payments money flow.

Also, seek a financial institution relationship which is focused on understanding and improving your business results.

In the fast changing world of payments an independent orchestrator can track innovations and periodically match your payments needs with the latest advances and performance in cards, Internet, Check 21 and the ACH world, as your business and your customers change as well.

Independent agents can also help you negotiate advantageous terms and conditions that protect your flexibility while increasing your profits. In addition, they can provide or recommend specialized resources for implementation and operations effectiveness of payments improvements.

Take Action

1. Use payments chain diagrams to visualize your situation.

2. Be aware that bundled solutions from captive agents may hide costs and restrict your flexibility to improve your payments systems to capture profits.

3. Find independent payments orchestrators to help, even if you have an excellent agent now.

More$Faster

www.paymentspower.com

3 USE SIMPLE AND CLEAR MEASUREMENTS

Two foundation metrics are defined for assessing payments systems profit opportunities and then measuring improvement.

The scope of **PAYMENTS POWER** includes both *In$ - money in,* and *Out$ - money out.*

The two dimensions of measurement are based on the relative amount and speed of usable money. These are *M$* for *In$*, and *L$* for *Out$, How Much*; and *F$, How Fast* for both.

Three strategies for unlocking profits are described:

1. **Improve** current payments practices.

2. **Switch** some payments to other types or other processing.

3. **Add** new payments choices to expand your mix of types and reduce costs and delays.

3 USE SIMPLE AND CLEAR MEASUREMENTS

You have two kinds of payments profit opportunities; **In$ - money in,** and **Out$ - money out,** and two dimensions of performance; *How Much,* **M$,** for **In$** with **L$** for **Out$,** and *How Fast,* **F$.** You can use these two sets of payments performance measurements to assess the current situation, compare payments types and then to measure improvements and spot trends over time - one pair for revenue, **In$**; and one pair for payments to employees and suppliers, **Out$.**

In$	All $ - Currency, Checks, Cards & Electronic Payments	
M$	**$ 96.51**	Usable $ from every $100 of Sales after <u>ALL</u> 'payments in' costs are subtracted
F$	**2.4 d**	Days from payment date until $ are usable in your deposit account

Payments Power *In$*

'Sales' is the primary source of money you send through payment systems or transport to your financial institution that will increase your usable balances. This includes all types of tender—paper currency and coin, paper checks, other paper money such as travelers checks and money orders; plastic cards of all types, credit, debit, gift and payroll, business purchasing cards, and fleet cards; and electronic payments such as incoming ACH, EDI and wire transfers, even trade credit sales.

The **M$** example shown in the figure above means that of every $100 of sales, this organization only ended up with of $96.51 of usable funds after subtracting all the payments systems costs.

The **F$** example time from the day of the sale to actually having use of the money was 2.4 business days. Because many obligations must be paid on a fixed schedule, such as payday, the timing of usable money is often critical. If the funds from sales are not available exactly when needed, either the money must be borrowed, liquid assets must be sold, or other planned uses of money must be delayed.

Payments Power Out$

The figure for **Out$** includes all types of payments you make—petty cash, paper checks, purchasing cards, direct deposit of payroll and taxes, online business bill payments, outgoing wire transfers, and any ACH origination to pay suppliers, contractors or employees.

L$ for moneys paid out represent the total of the payments and the payments systems costs. In this figure the $106.47 means for every $100 in payments to suppliers or employees, this company actually used nearly $107.

Out$	All $ - Currency, Checks, Cards & Electronic Payments	
L$	$106.47	Total $ used for every $100 paid after <u>ALL</u> 'payments out' costs are added
F$	5.4 d	Days from paid out date until usable $ are reduced in your deposit account

F$ for money paid out is like the mirror image of the delays you experience on available funds from sales—the 4.5 days in the example are counted from when you tender payment for goods or services until that payment actually reduces your available funds. For example, a contractor might perform repairs on your building's plumbing and present you a bill that day. If you pay by paper check, and the contractor deposits that check in his financial institution, which is not the same as your bank, the reduction in your usable account balance may not occur for one to five days. While the contractor marked your bill paid the day he got the check, you still had the use of the money for some business days longer. This is often called **float**.

A higher *F$* for *Out$* may be to your advantage. It depends, though. What if you were able to offer a more precise payment with lower costs to your supplier? Maybe then you could negotiate a discount on the goods and services that more than offset the advantage of the float.

How much and *how fast* are the two most important aspects of money flow. *M$, L$* and *F$* are simple measures of these payments performance dimensions.

Now let's consider three strategies, three paths to **PAYMENTS POWER**.

Payments Power Strategies

There are three key strategies that may significantly affect your future profits. Their effectiveness depends on information you have or will need to uncover about all types of payments; cash, checks, cards, and electronic transactions, and trade credit, if you use that.

1. **Improve.** Payments are so complicated that many organizations can increase profits just by changing policies and procedures with existing payments systems. Some simple actions can reduce payments costs up to or more than 100 basis points—that is 1% of revenue straight to the bottom line.

2. **Switch.** Change has been accelerating in payments technology and services for many years. Now the effect is so great you may be able to dramatically increase your profits by moving some portion of your transactions to a different, more efficient type of payment system. If you can recover 2.5% of revenue to add to an existing profit margin of 5% of sales, that would be a very exciting 50% profit improvement.

3. **Add.** You may even increase overall revenue on the same base of marketing and sales by offering your customers more payments choices. By adding the most advanced new methods you can im-

prove your operations, too. You might be able to handle much more sales volume without increasing your administrative overhead. This is more difficult to measure, but can bring a real boost to profit, even with some cost to implement the changes.

In the next chapter you will learn the first two critical steps to get started.

Take Action

Adopt two simple payments performance measures:

1. **M$** and **L$** for *How Much*

2. **F$** for *How Fast*

Examine both **In$ - money in,** and **Out$ - money out.**

Follow three payments performance improvement strategies;

1. **Improve** existing payments,

2. **Switch** some transactions to different, less costly types,

3. **Add** new payments choices for customers.

More$Faster

www.paymentspower.com

4 GET STARTED FAST

The first two steps are described and supported with two **PAYMENTS POWER** worksheets.

1. Begin by identifying the business units you should assess separately and the stores or locations you want to compare.

2. Next, complete the payments mix worksheets for each business unit and each location. One for ***In$ - money in*** and another worksheet for ***Out$ - money out*** as needed.

With these steps complete you can see the areas of most volume, but not yet set priorities for the first stage of improvements. That will require understanding your payments costs for the business units and the payments types you identified in these first two worksheets.

After completing the two starting steps you have the base to build on in the remaining chapters in **Part 1**.

You may use the second worksheet to also document your payments disbursed, though most readers will focus on payments received first.

4 GET STARTED FAST

How do you find out where you can improve profits and by how much?

First let's look at your kinds of customers and their payments mix. While you are doing that for payments coming in, you can also assess your profit opportunity hidden in payments going out.

> Various kinds of card payments are often underwritten with different merchant IDs (MIDs) due to different risks, average amounts and interchange classifications.

A common practice in credit card processing underwriting can be applied to all your incoming payments types. A retail store business that also has an Internet sales channel will almost always have a separate merchant ID for each of those sales channels.

In **PAYMENTS POWER** you will find that measuring these very different types of payment streams and all the associated payments costs will reveal where you should focus your profit improvement attention—and how you can tell if your efforts are paying off!

It is worthwhile separating lines of business if they experience very different payments characteristics:

1. Average transaction amount

2. Mix of tender

3. Delays in availability of money

4. Customers present or not at time of payment

5. Type of customer; consumer or business/government

The first worksheet is a visual checklist used to identify different kinds of payments businesses you will gather information on.

Here is a business example to help you see what I mean.

If the worksheet were completed for a tire business, retail would be checked for the stores where people drive in to get their tires replaced or fixed one vehicle at a time. The business-to-business or business-to-government (B2B/G) would be checked for the fleet business of the local county government.

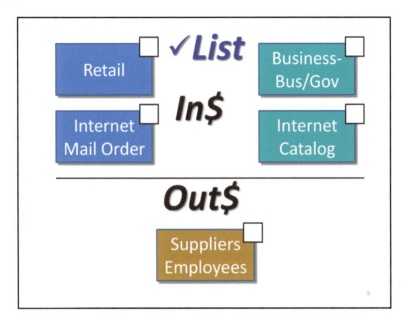

The tire business might also check the **Out$** box. Don't forget that every enterprise has some method, often several ways, to pay suppliers, contractors, employees, owners and investors. Your disbursements may be completely optimized, but if you think there may be some improvement possible you will want to measure and analyze the disbursements costs and then take action if the potential profit improvement is worthwhile.

You may want to do this for every store as well, especially if you measure to compare each store's performance.

Okay, what is next? You have to know your current situation. For each business unit or location complete the **Mix** column of the next worksheet. Calculate the percentage of money in the different payment types, not the percentage of number of transactions. Complete a worksheet for **In$** and another for **Out$** as needed. Do not worry yet about the last two columns. The steps to complete **M$** and **F$** columns for an **In$** worksheet, and likewise **L$** and **F$** for an **Out$** worksheet, will be covered in the rest of **Part 1**.

$Tender	Mix	M$	F$
Cash	%	$	d
Check	%	$	d
Card	%	$	d
ePay	%	$	d

In$ Worksheet (Out$ is similar with an L$ column instead of M$)

Your individual business units will likely show significant mix percentages variation by tender. Certainly, your **In$** and your **Out$** mix percentages will be very different.

Take Action

1. Identify your different business models and locations that should be separately analyzed.

2. Pick a time period; one or three months or a year.

3. Begin worksheets for **In$** and **Out$**, entering type of payments mix percentages – the percentage of money in cash, checks, cards and electronic payments.

5
Discover Profit Opportunities

Complete the high-level payments mix worksheets by adding the effect of payments costs and delays on **In$ - money in,** and **Out$ - money out**. Once these high-level worksheets are complete you can see where you should drill down in more detail.

You will calculate **M$** and **L$** for each payment type after estimating the associated payments cost components:

1. Fees - External costs

2. Expenses - Internal costs

3. Losses

You will identify the approximate delays in business days, **F$**.

For ongoing payments management there is an internal presentation of profit and loss to make your payments costs visible to your team.

Two examples of high-level worksheets are included based on payments research studies:

1. A study of payments mix in retail

2. A hypothetical B2B worksheet

5 DISCOVER PROFIT OPPORTUNITIES

The **PAYMENTS POWER** secrets are hidden in your income statement, probably below gross profit, not in cost of goods sold. You can use the framework to look for payments cost elements of fees, expenses, losses and time delays for **In$** and **Out$**.

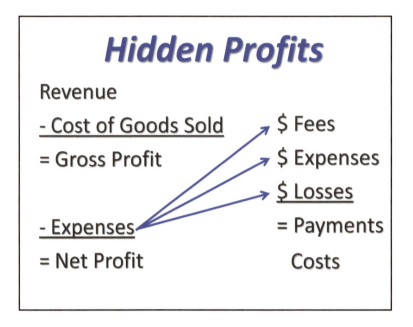

Chapters 6, 7 and 8 in **Part 1** will detail what you should look for in these three cost categories and how you might best use this information.

Once you have extracted or estimated all the payments systems costs, consider recasting a P&L statement for internal use that explicitly displays these costs for both payments in, **In$**, and payments out, **Out$**.

Otherwise your gross profit could be considered misleading because you do not get to use all your sales revenue. I suggest you consider subtracting **In$** payments costs before cost of goods sold to better calculate your actual gross profit, because these costs vary by sales amounts and number of transactions. Further, I recommend you separate the cost of payments out, **Out$**, from other expenses to focus attention of profit potential of payments systems. With this P&L visibility you can watch trends and measure payments improvements.

These figures are oversimplified, of course. This is management information, facts for decision making. This is not meant to comply with Generally Accepted Accounting Principles (GAAP), nor U.S. Securities and Exchange Commission (SEC) or other accounting standards. This is about profit improvement, not external reporting. For real accounting advice, go to a professional.

Visible Payments

Revenue

- Cost of *In$*

- Cost of Goods Sold

= Gross Profit

- Cost of *Out$*

- Remaining Expenses

= Net Profit

Payments Costs Sources

You will analyze your bank statements and merchant services statements to identify payments costs by type of payment in enough detail to uncover profit opportunities.

You are likely to find it difficult to analyze your credit card statements, but maybe even more challenging to extract *M$* and *F$* from your bank statements because *In$* and *Out$* fees and transaction volumes are all mixed together.

To classify bank payments costs and assess delays for money in and money out, you may need to follow transactions across three kinds of reports or file downloads monthly.

1. Account Analysis Statement

2. Daily Transactions, Deposits and Withdrawals

3. Daily Balances, collected and unavailable

The cost information on an analysis statement is likely to be grouped by currency and coin, checks, ACH, wire transfers, etc. Costs for money in are intermingled with costs for money out. The next figure illustrates how you will want to separate the costs, total deposits and total withdrawals and delays identified as uncollected funds or float.

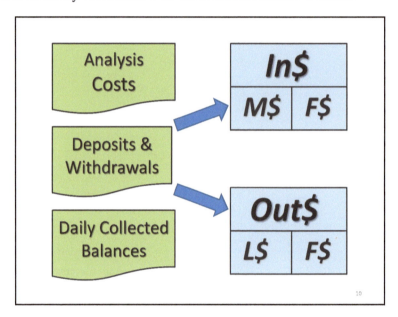

You may have to construct the **M$, L$** and **F$** for **In$** and **Out$** for each checking account if you have several and then roll up to results based on your organization structure.

For example, we analyzed a real estate office that has two broker locations, each with separate operating, escrow and commission accounts; a title company with operating and escrow accounts; and two property management offices each with escrow and operating accounts. They also accept credit card payments at the brokerage offices.

To manage payments performance they roll up two levels. The figure below illustrates the idea of **M$** and **F$** at the account level and the organizational unit level. In addition to profits and cash flow improvement, the broker has found a recruiting advantage in direct deposit of commission payments for agents, instead of paper checks.

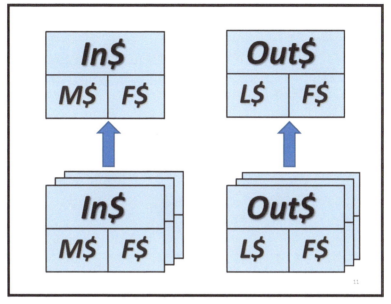

In$ and Out$ Payments Costs

Some payments costs may be deducted before your sales revenue is deposited, so you do not even get to use it temporarily. This has been a practice in merchant services for many years, but you can usually request that all sales revenue be deposited day by day with only a monthly ACH charge to your bank account for payments processing costs.

Let's see how you can reveal the secret opportunity.

Show me the money!

This worksheet is your complete money picture summary. You will complete two tables, one for *In$* and one for *Out$*.

You will want to extract the *In$* and *Out$* related information from your financial records, statements from your payments processors and your financial institution to subtract from revenue to calculate the money you actually have available to cover costs of goods sold, operating and other overhead expenses...And net profit. Remember, payments costs reductions will go straight to the bottom line.

$Tender	Mix	M$	F$
Cash	%	$	d
Check	%	$	d
Card	%	$	d
ePay	%	$	d

In the previous chapter, you learned to complete the mix column. Here you should complete estimates for the remaining worksheet columns. Even if the numbers are not precise, you will be able to prioritize further analysis time and effort. Let me repeat - When you complete these tables you will reveal your payments strengths and weaknesses. You will find where to focus payments improvements to unlock the greatest profits.

You will use cost detail to estimate $M\$$, the measure introduced in Chapter 2. Follow these steps for each $M\$$ cell for each type of tender received:

1. Pick a period; last month, last three months or last year.

2. Make a quick estimate of all your payments in, $In\$$, costs, including fees, expenses and losses such as uncollected returned checks or chargebacks.

3. Divide the total payments costs by your total sales for the same period.

4. Multiply by 100 to convert to dollars.

5. Subtract from $100, and enter into the worksheet.

6. Compare sales dates with collected funds dates on your bank statements to approximate $F\$$.

In$ Example Summary—Retail

Here is a **In$** summary that shows the national average payments mix from a 2008 study of retail stores; 29% of customer payments were currency and coin, 8% were paper checks, card payments including debit, credit and gift cards made up 63%. Because this example is from the retail store study there was no ePay tendered.

There will always be differences in **M$** and **F$** by type of money tendered.

The 2008 retail study provided the **Sales Mix** data for this table. I put in fictitious example numbers for **M$** and **F$** to illustrate how the worksheet can help focus profit improvement efforts. Later in the chapter, consider how the worst case scenarios can affect **M$** and **F$.**

In$	Sales Mix	M$	F$
Cash	29 %	$99.23	1.2d
Check	8 %	$98.51	2.1d
Card	63%	$97.32	3.2d
ePay	0 %	$0	0 d

What payment rows would you focus on in the figure to capture the most profits and accelerate available funds?

The answer seems obvious. Cards are the most important in retail overall, but you will have to drill down to determine specific opportunities and actions using other worksheets.

In card payments there are significant differences in total payments costs between *Present* and *Not Present*, credit cards and debit cards; and also between PIN and signature debit. These costs and delays contain your opportunities for profit improvement and accelerated funds in card payments.

Interchange has a fixed fee and a variable percentage per transaction. Just for MasterCard and Visa the range of interchange rates go from less than 1% with no fixed fee to over 3% and for some large transactions the fixed fee and other costs exceed $40. Other costs of your card payments processing may also have fixed and variable components. If you cannot find the detail in your current card statements, you may want to change processors. You will need the detail to track down root causes for downgrades, such as no address/Zip code, or CVV2 number or missing B2B data like invoice number or purchase order number.

CreditCd	Mix	Cost%	M$
Amex %	%	$	
Visa %	%	$	
MC %	%	$	
Disc %	%	$	

Two worksheets let you drill down to the next levels for card payments.

1. Start by breaking out the mix of card brands from your merchant services monthly statements, but include credit card transactions only.

2. Next, look at your check card (also called debit card) transactions by breaking out PIN debit from signature debit on the next worksheet.

3. Use your judgment to assess what combinations of mix and cost indicate where you might have profit improvement opportunity.

Cost% in the figures above and below is the total effective cost for that brand. Because it is a percentage of the sales amount you can easily determine **M$** by subtracting the **Cost%** from $100. For example, a 3.05% **Cost%** for Amex would mean the Amex **M$** is $96.95.

While it is commonly thought that the total effective cost of American Express card transactions are higher, I have seen some cases where other card brands have higher payments costs. It depends on many factors.

DebitCd	Mix	Cost%	M$
VSig	%	%	$
MCSig	%	%	$
VPIN	%	%	$
MCPIN	%	%	$

This is the worksheet for assessing signature and PIN check card transactions. If you have never looked at costs this way you may be surprised at the range of the variation in your payment processing costs.

Delays in receiving usable funds are important too. So, I recommend you estimate **F$**, the average number of days it takes to get available funds in your bank account. You may have to dig into your reconciliations of daily sales to bank deposits—this can be even harder to uncover than the hidden payment costs. Or ask your bookkeeper to give you estimates of the time delays.

Remember, the day funds are available may be one or more days after the date of deposit on the bank statement.

Out$	Mix	L$	F$
Cash	%	$	d
Check	%	$	d
Card	%	$	d
ePay	%	$	d

Out$

Follow these steps for each **L$** cell for each type of tender paid out and each kind of payment you use:

1. Pick a period; last month, last three months or last year.

2. Make a quick estimate of all your payments out, **Out$,** costs, including fees, expenses and losses.

3. Divide the total payments costs by your total payments disbursed for the same period.

4. Multiply by 100 to convert into dollars.

5. Add to $100 and enter into the worksheet.

6. Compare accounts payable paid dates to the withdrawal dates on your bank statements to approximate **F$**.

After you complete these tables you can easily see where your greatest **PAYMENTS POWER** opportunities lie, or where to drill down deeper.

B2B Out$ Research

Here is the example from the business-to-business world. While there is substantial purchasing card and other business credit card activity, and some electronic payments, the bulk of B2B remittance is still by paper check after receiving trade credit invoices.

This worksheet is an example of a B2B analysis pattern. Focus on the check payment type to discover hidden profit improvement opportunities.

Out$	Paid Mix	L$	F$
Cash	2%	$102.35	2.4d
Check	80 %	$112.14	2.4d
Card	11 %	$102.51	2.4d
ePay	7 %	$101.03	1.4d

Next, let's review some scenarios you might find.

Perfect In$—100% Money Today

Here is a target condition: All your revenue money is deposited in the bank account and available the same day as the sale. Even more perfect - All revenue money, *In$,* is in the bank account before any money is spent, *Out$,* to produce the product or service sold—the PC direct online business model where they take payment before building your computer. This is not just high inventory turns, but negative inventory turns.

Are you in this state of grace today? If so, I want to hear your story!

Reality. Payments processors and financial institutions are very important service suppliers, and rightfully earn fees for their services which take some time to complete and settle, and for underwriting payments risks. Businesses and non profits that rely on payments services just want reasonable costs and understandable payments information.

Worst Case - 60% Less Money Only Available After 30 to 40 Days

Here is the other end of the spectrum. For a hundred dollars sold, you find only $40 in your bank account, and it gets deposited 30 to 40 days after the payment for your goods or services. Would you put up with this? Is any of your sales money in this deplorable condition?

I am talking about returned checks—not fraud, just checks tendered by your customers that were returned due to insufficient or uncollected funds.

Every enterprise is different, but national averages show ½ of 1% of checks accepted are returned, and up to 60% of face value is written off, and the 40 % of face value that is collected takes an average of 30 to 40 days.

If your business takes checks and some are returned, you may want to learn about how easy it is to get the face value of 80% to 85% of your non-sufficient funds (NSFs) collected in seven to fifteen days—*for free (Sort of)*, and eliminate most of your operations costs of telephone call collections, the hassle, and collections tracking.

I will tell you more about this fast acting profit secret, and give you some tips on why some solutions are better choices than others.

eCommerce - Up to 6% Less Money Available After two to three Days

You may find profit opportunity in your Internet business, especially if you use a gateway processor or accept a significant portion of PayPal payments. Be sure you find all the costs of the payments building blocks.

Most internet credit card business is deemed high risk—it is *Card*

Not Present, and often is characterized by future delivery of products, another risk factor.

Some people we have talked to have reported total payments costs for Internet sales as high as 5% to 6% of revenue. Are you an Internet-based business, or do you have a growing portion of revenue from on-line sales?

You may have margins so good this doesn't bother you. But, we recommend you explore ways to reduce the payments costs of Internet sales if they are above 3% of revenue. At least you should measure and track the gap and delays between sales and actual dollars.

> Maybe you have net profit of 20% of Internet sales. Would 21% be better? That's a 5% profit increase!

Perfect Out$ - 100% Money the Precise Day You Pick to Pay

Paying suppliers exactly when you want to is a deeply ingrained supply chain preference. But, your improvement goals for vendor management might also include increasing quality, price, terms or on-time delivery. Committing to more precise, predictable payments and funds availability for your suppliers can advance all these goals. Meanwhile you can also execute **Out$** at lowest internal expense and with competitive external payments processing fees.

Would this be ideal? What do you think? I want to know your story.

Worst Case - Less than 50% Certainty in Payment Effective Dates

Do you miss any important supplier payments commitments resulting in deteriorating, even adversarial relationships?

Do you continually use your suppliers to finance your working capital, but also suspect you get the *least favorite customer* level of support?

Are there hidden costs in the unreliable supply of important materials and services?

Check the trade-offs you are making today. There may be some profit improvement opportunity in revising your policy and practice of paying as late as possible, but with paper checks and unpredictable mail delivery. Look into using more precise electronic payments.

First, assess your costs. Then you can focus your improvement actions.

Take Action

1. Estimate payments costs to complete the worksheet *M$* and *L$* columns.

2. Estimate payments delays to complete the *F$* columns.

3. Drill down to further sharpen focus and priorities.

4. Decide how you will keep payments performance visible to see trends, and for continuous improvement.

5. Prioritize areas for more extensive analysis.

6 Discover *In$* Costs

For the *In$* payment types that have the lowest estimated *M$*, you may wish to refine your measurements of payments costs. This chapter starts with descriptions of three categories of payments costs, an explanation of delays and some further trade credit insight.

Delays are described in more detail to refine the *F$* assessment.

This chapter gives examples that can help you see a more complete and accurate picture of cost reduction opportunities for different payment types.

Three stories illustrate real world situations in the chapter:

1. Discourage Checks

2. Payment Plan

3. Card Returns

Also included are two payments chains used to help analyze costs and delays:

1. Card Not Present

2. Online Bill Payment

6 Discover *In$* Costs

This chapter includes specific examples of four areas of opportunity including three categories of payments costs plus the hidden profit leakage from delays in available funds. As you look for these payments costs you may find other payments waste too. You should gather information over at least a three month period on fees, expenses, losses and delays for all payments coming in.

You will want to choose the level of detail. Just as in any business analysis, the cost of research can exceed potential savings. Payments analysis is full of pennies and basis points per transactions, seemingly trivial amounts of money.

Perhaps that is why so few business people devote much attention to payments, but the profit opportunity adds up when you multiply those seemingly trivial pennies and basis points by all your affected payments amounts and transactions volumes.

Once you have a useful baseline of payments costs, no matter the level of detail, be sure that you can compare your *M$* and *F$* over time. Seeing change from month to month and quarter to quarter, good or bad, is critical to managing your payments systems to improve profits.

To help identify and follow payments costs you should sort them by category.

Fees

These payments costs are paid to outside suppliers of products and services. They may collect directly from your account or even by reducing your daily deposits from sales. Or you may pay by bill payment or check. These costs are usually easy to identify even if difficult to understand.

Expenses

Internal costs of handling *In$* are soft costs, meaning that even if you improve a process you do not automatically improve profit. Sure, there can be substantial benefits from reducing work by improving a payments process, then moving people to other value add processes. Quantifying and then reducing these soft costs is challenging.

> If you use product and service target costing in research and development, you might ask yourself if expected payments costs and delays are part of your design. Should you include these costs?

Losses

These payments costs are easier to find. The accounting systems will reveal write-offs that reduce assets or income. You might classify payments risk mitigation as this type of cost. For example, services such as check verification and guarantee replace the uncertainty of a large bad check loss with a smaller, predictable cost assessed against every check accepted.

Delays

Waiting to receive payment is easy to understand, but usually not measured precisely or tracked over time for all payments. The lag time between the day of a sale and the availability of funds in your business checking account can cause significant costs if your business is tight on money. This is the cost of using other sources of funds when you cannot wait to receive the money from sales. These costs may come from borrowing, raising capital, or selling assets such as factoring receivables.

Payday always arrives, and if you do not have some significant part of your most recent sales in the bank you may have to borrow money to cover payroll. Some calculate the cost of float, delays in payments availability, using the interest cost of borrowing, while others use their weighted average cost of capital. Because interest costs and cost of capital vary over time, I recommend using *F$* measured in days for tracking delay trends; faster or slower availability.

B2B Trade Credit

Business-to-business or business-to-government companies commonly offer sales terms to their customers, such as payment 30 days from invoice or sales date, with discounts for earlier payment, or penalties for later payment.

This extension of credit, identified as trade credit in payments chain tender, increases both **F$** and expense payments costs.

The *faster* part of the mantra and my purpose is not only about the accounting measure of Days Sales Outstanding (DSO). DSO is used in enterprises to assess efficiency of collecting accounts receivable balances, trade credit extended to buyers. DSO is for credit sales only though, and does not reveal the full picture of Delay cost of all types of payments.

DSO is commonly defined as the ending total receivables divided by total credit sales for the period, times the number of days in the period. A DSO benchmark of ten to fifteen days longer than the nominal term of the sale is considered good for converting accounts receivables into bank account balances on the general ledger. Depending on the nominal payments terms, DSO could range from 10 to 30 to 90 days or more.

DSO is a good tool calculated on the internal accounting system, but typically does not include the timing gap between the internal accounting bank account posting date and when the deposits become available, usable funds in your financial institution account. That gap can and should be measured in addition to DSO and can be reduced to accelerate cash flow. **F$** is a measure of that gap for all payments types, including trade credit sales.

There are two primary elements of the gap. The first is daily deadlines for deposits earlier than the end of day for an enterprise – 2:00 pm at many financial institutions for branch deposits of checks and cash. Second, if you do not close credit card batches by the daily deadline you will see an extra day delay and incur downgrading costs as well.

The second element is simply the time to process and clear the transactions. We are all familiar with the notion that our financial institution may not give immediate or same day available credit to deposited checks unless they are drawn on the same institution. It takes additional steps and time to collect a check drawn on another institution, even if the transaction is cleared electronically through some of the payments chain.

F$ days is the measure for this gap.

Cash-Currency and Coin

Even cash has payments costs. If you accept any volume of currency and coin you may be paying for counting and coin wrapping and currency strapping and armored car transport.

Why do grocery stores encourage *Cash Back*? Because otherwise they have to protect, count and transport more currency and coin before they get collected funds in their bank accounts. This book will detail how to get more money faster out of cash and check deposits.

You may be able to take advantage of innovations like the smart safe vaults services that accelerate the funds availability of currency and coin deposits. There is likely a cost trade-off, though—be sure to carefully identify the costs of these services and compare to your existing cash payments costs and delays.

In$ Cash	
Fees	Count and Wrap
	Armored Car
	Safe Vault
	Foreign Exchange
Expenses	Deposit Prep
	Security
	Onsite ATM
	Manage
Losses	Over and Short
	Counterfeit
Delays	Next Day Deposits

Some stores have outsourced a portion of their currency costs with in-store automated teller machines (ATMs). Measure the processing costs even if you receive offsetting ATM fee sharing revenue.

Exchange

If you are being paid by customers with foreign currency you may also find substantial fees for currency exchange. More on this subject in Chapter 13.

Cash Over and Short

Currency and coin shrinkage can be a problem for some enterprises. Robbery and theft, while rare, can substantially reduce the actual money harvested from cash sales. The expenses of physical security are a cost of this payment type too. With currency payments there is sometimes the risk of a dishonest cashier not ringing up sales—the inventory or service is delivered, but no revenue is gained.

If someone is personally carrying large amounts of cash and checks to and from your financial institution you are risking and perhaps experiencing theft, personal danger or productivity loss as well. Do you have additional costs to protect your people and cash in transit?

Counterfeit

If you accept currency and make change for larger bills as many retail enterprises do, you may suffer some losses from accepting bogus bills. Training and procedures for handling large denomination bills are a cost of cash sales that might be classified either as an Expense or under Loss, as a risk management expenditure.

Checks-Deposits Prep and Transport

I will bet most of you have seen or done the work of opening envelopes to process payment checks and bills, or added up a stack of checks taken at sales registers to complete a bank account deposit. Then someone drives the deposit to the nearest branch.

Or, you pay an armored car service to pick up your check deposits and excess currency and coin, or to deliver replenishments for cash drawers. All this expense is in support of generating sales or converting sales into usable money in the bank account.

Some of the costs are direct fees for outside services and some are internal resource costs. Even if you have moved to an electronic conversion of paper checks, you can identify the costs of that approach.

Financial Institution Fees

In addition to financial institution charges for deposits received, you may pay one time and ongoing costs for desktop deposit - to scan and deposit check images and payment data. Also called RDC, Remote Deposit Capture, this self service capability can save time and money over transporting checks to a financial institution branch, but be sure you understand all the costs of desktop deposit, scanning error rates and even intangibles like *green* impact.

In$ Check	
Fees	Check Verify
	Lockbox Service
	Desktop Deposit
	Check Conversion
Expenses	Self - operated Lockbox
	NSF Collecting
	Accounts Receivable–Invoices, state - ments, and NSF handling
	Branch Deposit
Losses	Check Guarantee
	Collection Agency
	NSF Write Off
	Fraud/Forgery
Delays	Next Day Deposits
	Check Clearing
	Invoice Terms

Cutoff Times and Check 21 Deposits

If you receive a significant number of check payments, you will be concerned about collecting these funds quickly. Even with a modest volume you might want to verify the amounts and lag time of this portion of your revenue.

Delays and cost of transporting checks received are being eliminated by using remote deposit to scan and transmit individual payment information. Deposit deadlines are extended with remote deposits, too. If you are making branch deposits, be sure you measure the delays in collected funds related to late day sales receipts that have to wait until the next business day deposit.

There are second generation desktop check deposit solutions available from financial institutions and independent payments processors for reducing cost and speeding electronic check collections.

Later in the book we will examine desktop deposit in more detail. The costs and reduction of delays of electronic deposit should also be understood and included in your analysis framework.

NSF Collections, Disputes and Losses

Expenses to collect NSF checks by phone and mail can be measured or estimated. While some of the other payments costs or delays may require estimates, or educated guesses, the write off of NSF checks not collected should be easy to measure.

Forgeries

Bogus Travelers checks, stolen business checks, altered check amounts—these are especially costly because you lose all the revenue and you have to spend more to recover any goods you sold, if you can.

Over the years payments systems have added protections such as anti-tampering features on check paper, but just knowing your customers and checking identification are still good practices to control these costs. Do you count all these activities as part of your check payments systems costs? They are usually very visible and gain plenty of attention.

Checks vs. Card Not Present Story

To avoid the waste of collecting bounced checks Frank's business follows a policy of accepting payments by card or cash only. This is disclosed on the initial sign-in document the customer completes to provide information the business uses to properly match service to the customer's needs.

Most transactions are face to face, but some reservations are made weeks in advance. To hold the reserved block of days, the first day is paid over the phone. The remainder is paid in person at check-out time.

For the card not present transactions over a four month period the Visa effective cost was 3.49% and MasterCard was 3.52%.

So, out of every $100 first day reservation sales, after payments costs the business was left with only $96.50 in usable money.

How much more usable money would have been realized if Frank was able to accept ACH - based electronic checks by phone?

Cards

Authorization and Capture

Authorization is the real-time process that brings such value to accepting card payments. Standalone terminals, point of sale applications, personal computer virtual terminals and Internet gateways can all provide this. Authorization fees are an important component of card payments cost you should understand and measure. You may have to look in more than one processing statement to find all these costs. Look at terminal fees such as rental and supplies, too.

Card Settlement Processing

A big money improvement opportunity is often found in plastic card payments settlement. Big law suits have arisen from the imbalance in power reflected in non-negotiable interchange pricing from Master-Card/Visa, Discover and American Express. Some of the rules that were challenged restricted merchants from using lower cost payments with their customers. To take advantage of the opportunity you need to assess and determine if you can and should shift some card transactions to lower cost alternatives.

The advantage of authorized credit card or debit card transactions may be more than offset by the interchange fees, plus processing and gateway fees that are deducted from your sales revenue.

If you are like most decision makers you get calls from merchant services sales representatives nearly every week. They promise to cut your processing costs if you will switch to their solution. Guess what, your big profit opportunity in credit card processing is not in the processing fees. It is in understanding and managing, to the extent you can, interchange costs.

If you do switch, read your existing and proposed contracts carefully. You should try to avoid large penalties for early contract termination, and watch out for 'evergreen' clauses and long pre-cancelation notification periods. Know how much in advance of the contract renewal date you have to notify of your intention to switch processors to avoid any significant penalty.

In the Discourage Checks story earlier in the chapter the total effective cost of the telephone card not present transactions was about 3.5% of sales revenue.

The story is an example of a very difficult analysis of the merchant services statement that was required to clearly separate and assign on a common sense basis payments costs to different types of card transactions.

Let's look next at the payments chain for a card not present transaction. The difference is key entry instead of card swipe. After capture this shows the same payments processing as card present transactions.

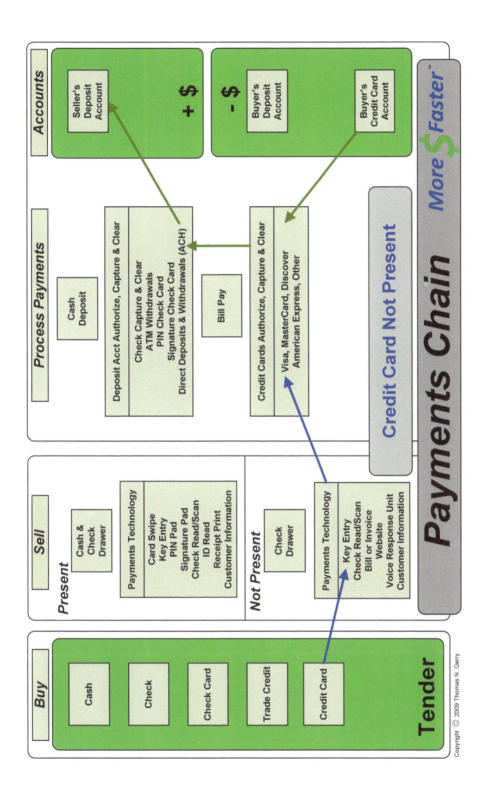

65

It costs more because of higher interchange rates for card not present classifications.

Many decisions about accepting card types have been made based on perceived payments cost. Yet research shows that customer satisfaction and higher sales have been identified with more payments choices.

Consider also the demographic preferences of your primary customer profile; high tech, senior, youth, and millennium segments.

Interchange

The complexity of the card payments systems' rules, and the layering of fees for Internet payments, gateway and perhaps PayPal make this aspect of your payments most important to understand and measure to get more money faster. Here is a story to illustrate this point.

Payment Plans Story

If a customer requests a payment plan over several months to cover the cost of an expensive surgery procedure, Mary, the office manager, can offer an installment payment agreement the customer signs.

The initial installment is processed with the card and customer present, but the remaining installments are all 'card not present' transactions, which incur much higher payments cost, as much as 1% of revenue or greater above 'card present' interchange and processing costs.

Analysis of three months merchant processing statements revealed that overall this business, despite delivering services face to face, has only 40% qualified card transactions. The credit card installment payment plans generate a significant number of unqualified card not present transactions. An alternative approach is worth investigating.

It is especially important to understand and measure the *Card Not Present* charges separately because these transactions are good candidates for changes that will improve profits.

Card Returns Story

The TotalCareXpress dental services provided could be quite expensive—the average transaction was over $500, and some totaled more than $1,000 for services and goods. Returns were 6% of total credit card sales.

A private label credit application form is provided right at the check-out counter for customers that want these particular expenses on a separate credit card account offering no interest financing for 24, 36, 48 and 60 month initial promotional periods.

However, to ensure the care needed is delivered quickly, a branded credit card transaction is processed at check in based on an estimate of the expected total cost of the procedures and drugs.

After the services are performed a credit is processed if the initial charge was too high. But the greatest amount of returns occurs when the private label credit accounts are approved and the original transactions are refunded in total, and the new account is charged instead.

But here is the really bad news. Even though Visa and MasterCard require refunding most of the interchange on transactions that are credited, the card processor not only did not return the refunded interchange money, they charged another processing fee on the refund transactions. So, the business pays processing fees three times, and interchange two times; first on the original branded card payment, second on the private label charge!

> Guess what, your big profit opportunity in credit card processing may not be in the processing fees. It is in understanding and managing, to the extent you can, interchange costs.

What if a credit card charge is disputed and reversed, for any reason? Whether you are processing under tiered discount pricing, where your statements show qualified, mid and non-qualified transaction classifications; or interchange cost plus, you should measure how much of your revenue is being classified as more costly interchange transactions, often called downgrading, or up charging.

CyberSource reports that 5% of Internet card transactions are downgraded for reasons you may be able to fix. They say the cost improvement can range from 0.45% to 2% of the payment amount (45 to 200 basis points).

This requires the audit of your statements and perhaps sampling actual payment processes in your stores or your back office.

Innovations

Watch for developments in consumer credit cards such as the Revolution Card which replaces hundreds of interchange categories with a single fixed percentage network clearing charge. Even with authorization and capture and settlement processor fees, the total *In$* cost is dramatically lower than the *In$* costs of Visa, MasterCard, and the other well-known credit card payments choices.

In addition, with the Revolution Card there is no built in cost bias against smaller average transactions that is part of most credit card interchange formulas.

American Express has announced an agreement to acquire Revolution Card. We will watch to see if this will become a major competitive move in the payments industry.

'Pal Charges'

If your Internet business payments include PayPal or one of their competitors, you will want to assess all their fees that reduce your sales deposits. Look for more detail in Chapter 12.

Losses - Chargebacks

Likewise, credit card charge backs (not returns, but cases where the service is consumed or the product is used and kept) should be easily determined from the processing statements. What may cause you some difficulty is that some credit card chargeback interchange costs are different than the original transactions interchange fees.

If you have an Internet business you will have noticed the emergence of fraud filters and fraud prevention technologies in response to more and more sophisticated criminal attacks from around the world.

Check out payer authentication online such as Verified by Visa and MasterCard SecureCode which can reduce fraud and even shift fraud liability back to the issuing bank.

Losses—Payment Card Industry Compliance Penalties Risk

We are all aware of the reports of thefts of thousands of credit card numbers and names. We see and hear ads about identity theft and protection. The card associations have strengthened their security requirements of payments participants and components of the payments chains.

Simply put, you may have to pay serious financial penalties if credit card account information is stolen as a result of your enterprise not taking care to protect the private customer information of name and account number on credit cards.

So, do your own audit of how you store and dispose of customer names and associated card account numbers. Set up an education and certification process to document and deploy your policy and procedure for payment card industry (PCI) compliance. You have probably been notified of this requirement by your card processor, but you should know there is the possibility of large penalties, potentially thousands of dollars, if a problem is traced back to your noncompliance.

Check your merchant processing statements to see if you are paying monthly fees that you do not understand, such as a fee for not being PCI compliant.

Some payments processors are buying insurance to cover potential costs of a data breach, including the forensic audit and any penalties. Find out if your processor is covered.

You may want to have your team extend this beyond just cards. Paper and electronic checks also contain potentially vulnerable customer name, address and account numbers—for individuals as well as for B2B customers.

Go to the Internet for more background. And expect this concern and risk to continue developing. Crime prevention requires continual improvement. The bad guys keep thinking up new ways to steal. Remember, customer payment information is one of the primary targets – protect it diligently!

Delays - Chargeback Reserves

When merchant processors see chargeback experience greater than ½%, they may act to mitigate credit risk by reducing your deposit amounts and holding some of your revenue in reserve perhaps 30 to 60 days or longer in case of disputes resulting in return of payments. Your *F$* goes longer, and your *M$* may be reduced.

In$ ePay	
Fees	Processing
Expenses	Enter and Reconcile
	Dispute Defense
	Manage
Losses	Chargebacks
Delays	Payment Day vs. Usable Money Day

Electronic Payments

More and more payments are received as electronic transactions. Let's look at one of the most used—online bill payment. Your customer, the buyer, receives a bill or invoice and elects to use their bank or accounting system bill payment capability. Their bill payment processor sends ACH transactions (or a substitute paper check) to directly withdraw money on the effective date from the buyer's financial account and deposit the funds in the seller's depository account.

As the seller where are your costs? You may pay a third party or you may generate your own bills and invoices. You may have to spend extra time to determine how to update your accounts payable records if the electronic payments do not clearly identify which bill or invoice line item is being paid. The buyer may not be able to pay as fast because of the bill pay effective date lag—often three to five days.

Take a look at the Payments Chain diagram on the following page that shows an online bill payment flow.

ePay Chargebacks

ACH charge backs will likely grow as ACH transaction volume continues its dramatic trend upward. Just as with credit card charge backs, you may suffer losses without the offset of returned goods that might be resold. The following payments chain indicates the money is taken from the buyer's deposit account by ACH, but sometimes this is done with a substitute paper check generated by the bill pay processor. The paper check may take longer to clear for the seller.

Financial Institution Accounts In$ Costs and Speed

Your bank or credit union may charge for each check received, each deposit of cash and checks, wire transfer fees and each ACH deposit transaction posted.

So, in addition to the payments costs from payments chain authorization and capture processors, you may also pay again as the funds are received by your financial institution. For example, on credit card payments your total costs include online authorization, payment capture and settlement, interchange to the issuing banks, and finally perhaps a charge for the ACH deposit of your day's credit card sales receipts.

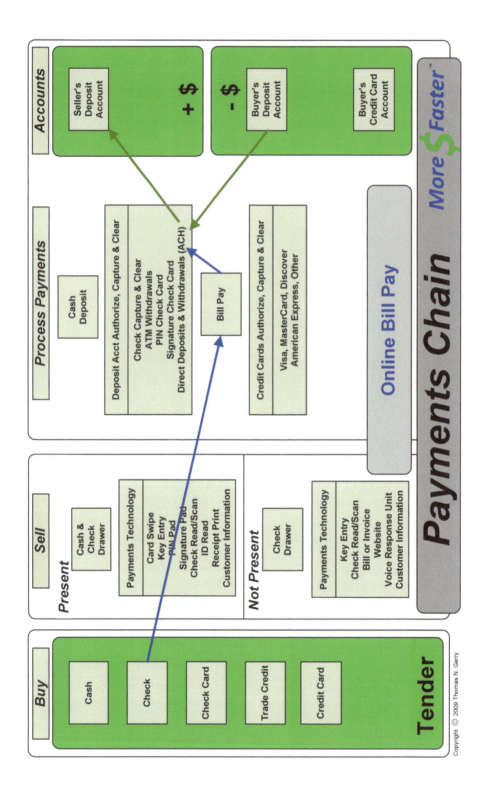

If your enterprise maintains high enough balances and uses a range of bank services, your business checking may be designated for Account Analysis. Hard and soft charges are detailed on monthly statements and pro forma interest on average collected balances is used to offset some or all the charges. If you are in that state month after month it seems like you have lower or no costs for checking transactions—but the opportunity cost of not investing those deposits elsewhere is real even if not an actual expense that affects your P&L.

Follow these steps to measure your payments in, *In$*, costs and speed, *F$*, for the financial institution:

In$

1. Identify on your bank statements the total monthly deposit transactions.

2. Separate the individual costs for *In$* transactions into cash, checks, cards and ePay worksheets. (Deposits for cards will be ACH transactions, and ePay *In$* will include ACH and wire transfers.)

3. Exclude account to account cash management transfers that are not *In$* payments related.

4. Decide how to allocate non transaction monthly fees and add to the worksheets.

F$

1. Identify deposits by date in your point of sale systems or accounting records.

2. On the bank statements identify the corresponding dates of deposit.

3. On the available funds statements determine the additional days and amounts held as unavailable.

4. Calculate the *F$*, the number of days from sale until usable funds in the account, for each payment type and update the worksheets.

This chapter has helped you drill down where needed on *In$* payments costs and related *F$* delays. Now with this information you can focus improvements and measure progress in profits gained as you tweak your payments systems.

That is, unless you finance your buyers' purchases with trade credit, the subject of the next chapter.

Take Action

In$ costs are hard to analyze due to confusing, perhaps misleading statements from some payments processors and financial institutions.

1. Separate and sort into three categories of *In$* costs – Fees, Expenses, and Losses.

   • Sharpen your analysis; make external fees visible to prioritize profit opportunity.

   • Be open to potential internal expense improvements where valuable.

   • Assign losses and loss mitigation expenses to each type of tender.

2. Gain insight to measure delays.

3. Prioritize the most profit and speed potential.

7 DISCOVER B2B TRADE CREDIT *In$* COSTS

For B2B sales to customers based on business relationships and internal credit decisions, you may wish to refine your measurements of *In$* payments costs and the effects of offering shorter or longer final payment terms. This chapter extends the **PAYMENTS POWER** framework for the widely used B2B trade credit practice.

Trade credit is explored in more detail, and broken into two distinct payments events for effective analysis and management.

These two steps are used to help analyze costs and delays:

1. Buyer Purchase on the day of the sale

2. Buyer Payment at 30, 60, 90 or more days later

7 DISCOVER B2B TRADE CREDIT
In$ COSTS

As noted in Chapter 2, trade credit is the most significant purchasing tender in B2B/G commerce. To assess payments costs of this practice, it is useful to examine and understand the two steps that are separated in time; the purchase and the subsequent related payment.

Step		Buyer Purchase	
		Debit	Credit
First	**Buyer**	**Expense or Asset**	**Accounts Payable**
		Debit	Credit
Sale Day	**Seller**	**Accounts Receivable**	**Revenue**

First Step

The first step is easy if the buyer has an established relationship with the seller. These relationships are the foundation of B2B commerce. Most business thrives and grows only because of the mutually beneficial sharing of information and risk. The relationship supports the granting of payment terms by the seller to the buyer.

While down payments and deposits may be required, the great portion of B2B purchases occurs with a promise to pay money in the future. The buyer's promise to pay is the tender on the day of the purchase, just as effective as cash, check, credit card or electronic payment for the buyer. Unfortunately for the seller, the accounts receivable, A/R, created by the sale is not as useful as the other forms of tender—it cannot be used to pay wages or buy supplies and services, A/R is a non-cash asset.

Second Step

The revenue credit reflects the sale transaction, but does not help cash flow that day. So, the delay from the first step, the purchase, to the second step, the money payment on the receivable is very important to management. Days Sales Outstanding, DSO, is a commonly used measure for accounts receivable to watch and improve. Improvement means reducing the number of days.

Step	Buyer Payment		
Second 30, 60, 90 + Days Later	Buyer	**Debit** Accounts Payable	**Credit** Cash
	Seller	**Debit** Cash	**Credit** Accounts Receivable

Competitive forces and opportunities may pull in the other direction, though. The business may win more sales, at higher margins if longer terms are offered. So, DSO reduction is limited by the market.

Beyond DSO, **F$** can and should be estimated for trade credit. I recommend you include the time from receipt of the buyer payment until the funds are usable in your bank account. This gap may be very short compared to the period from the sales day to receiving a check and posting the payment to accounts receivable.

This delay is worth costing and improving as well as standard DSO.

Take Action

1. B2B trade credit **In$** costs are hidden in the two payments steps separated by time.

   - Assess all your trade credit delays costs including Days Sales Outstanding, DSO, and from the day payment is received until funds are available to use

   - Include bad debt expense of trade credit invoices not collected in the checks losses cost category

2. Separate and sort into three categories of **In$** costs – fees, expenses, and losses.

3. Prioritize the highest profit and speed potential.

8 Discover *Out$* Costs

You will want to focus on more detail for the ***Out$*** payments types estimated to have the highest **L$.** This chapter gives examples that help you see a more complete and accurate picture of cost reduction opportunities by disbursement payments type.

In addition, delays are described in more detail to refine your **F$** assessment.

This chapter includes two stories of real world situations:

1. B2B Checks

2. Online B2B Bill Pay

Two payments chains are used to help analyze costs and delays visually:

1. Pay an Invoice with a Check

2. Online Bill Payment

8 DISCOVER *Out$* COSTS

There is a simple *Out$* objective—pay as late as you can without undo penalties or costs. There is advantage in understanding the payments chain costs of your suppliers—if you can solve some of their **PAYMENTS POWER** issues you may be able to negotiate lower prices for goods and services you purchase.

Here are some specific examples of three categories of hidden payments costs plus the delays in paying out funds. As you look for these payments costs you may find other payments waste too.

You should gather information over at least a 3 month period on fees, expenses, losses and delays for payments disbursed.

This chapter will spend a little time on cash, go through more detail on checks because B2B payments still are over 70% paper, with limited remarks on card payments, and finish with the fast growing electronic payments options.

We will use simple payments chain examples of a check payment and an online bill payment in response to an invoice received. These give a visualization of the flow of information and money. You can see where payments costs and delays occur, and you can identify supply chain partners' concerns in your choice of tender.

Let's start with physical cash.

Out$ - Currency and Coin

Do you have workers you must pay by cash, or do you cash payroll checks for your employees? If so, you may incur some of the payments costs listed in the following table.

Perhaps you pay with cash your people that do not have checking accounts because otherwise they would have to pay expensive check cashing fees. Those costs your workers suffer might be considered a hidden *Out$* cost because without those fees you might be able to pay less for the work.

Out$ Cash	
Fees	Counting and Wrapping
	Exchange
	Envelopes
Expenses	Approval
	Cash Drawer Counting
	Filling Envelopes
Losses	Over and Short
	Theft
	Dual Control
Delays	Inventory of Non-Earning Assets

Out$ - Exchange

If you are paying cross border affiliates or suppliers you may also find substantial fees for currency exchange. See Chapter 13 for more on this subject.

Out$ – Paper checks

Out$ expenses may be due to paying expense reimbursements and commissions with paper checks. Payments to suppliers and partners by paper checks may cost more money than electronic payments.

In small quantities business checks can cost up to $0.25 each and then you pay for the time and ink to print, and the envelop and postage to mail. I have seen studies that range from $2.50 to $12.50 per paper check, including labor, materials, and postage.

Other *Out$* payments costs to look for are wire transfer fees, and delivery costs of sending checks overnight.

Out$ Check	
Fees	Check Stock
	Postage
	Expedited Delivery
	Envelopes
Expenses	Printing
	Approval
	Signing and Review
	Stuffing
	Late Payment Discussions
	File Uploading
Losses	Stolen Checks
	Altered Checks
	Positive Pay Costs
Delays	Approval and Review
	Delivery Variation
	Lead Time to Avoid Late Payment
	Clearing After Receipt

Out$ - Financial Institution Fees

Your bank may charge for each check withdrawal, ACH withdrawal transaction posted and wire transfers out. You may also be paying additional risk mitigation costs for 'Positive Pay' and automated account reconciliation for check payments.

Positive Pay prevents payment of bogus business checks by matching clearing transactions against disbursement files uploaded from enterprise accounts payable activity. If there is not a match with the control file, the item is rejected and returned. Financial institutions charge for the service, so this might be one of your payments costs for checks.

If your enterprise has enough balances and a range of services, your business checking may be designated for account analysis. Hard and soft charges are enumerated on monthly statements and pro forma interest on maintained balances is used to offset some or all the charges.

If you are in that state month after month it seems like you have no costs for checking payments—but the opportunity cost of not investing those deposits elsewhere is real even if not an hard charge by the bank.

B2B Checks Story

The Great Northern trucking company pays most suppliers by check. Mr. Dave, the founding patriarch, looks at every check going out and sometimes pulls one out to be researched.

Is the payee valid? Is the amount correct? Did we authorize the purchase? Did we receive the goods or services? Do we owe the payment now? Dave's controller has two clear goals—pay bills as close to the date due as possible, and keep usable bank balances as long as possible.

The accounts payable department prepares and mails checks five days before due. Unfortunately, some of the payments still arrive past the due date. Because the company is very sound and reliable, typically a phone call is all that is needed to explain the late payment and avoid a penalty. Sometimes the reason offered is the uncertainty of mail delivery. These phone calls are a waste, a cost which may be difficult to calculate precisely, but is very real.

The other consequence of mailing paper checks five days in advance is that many payments are early, and this variation reduces available balances earlier than desired.

Out$ - Forgeries

Stolen business checks and altered check amounts can result in **Out$** losses. An operations executive at a hotel properties management company that pays suppliers for linen service, food service and miscellaneous hotel costs told me that they often find bogus checks clearing their checking account.

If they were not reconciling their disbursements diligently, their payments out costs, **L$**, could be much higher. Financial institutions can help with this, but also at an additional cost.

Payments Chain Example

Let's look at a payments chain for a check paid in response to an invoice received. We can see each step, including what we do, what the seller does and what the payments processors do. If you consider the variation in the process steps you can assess the waste caused by some payments being late and others early.

Use the **Out$ Check** table to identify elements of payments costs and delays and risk of loss as you go through the process steps of the payments chain.

Look for opportunity to improve your supply chain partners' profits too. That can be a way to negotiate better terms, perhaps even lower prices.

You may find lots of technologies and approaches used by your most important trading partners. Around the world businesses and nonprofit organizations are improving their receivables and payable processes and reducing waste. Many payments processing improvements may be found in other industries.

This book is deliberately **not** written for just a selected vertical market. I believe you may find new ideas here you can apply, even if the story or tip is from an entirely different kind of enterprise.

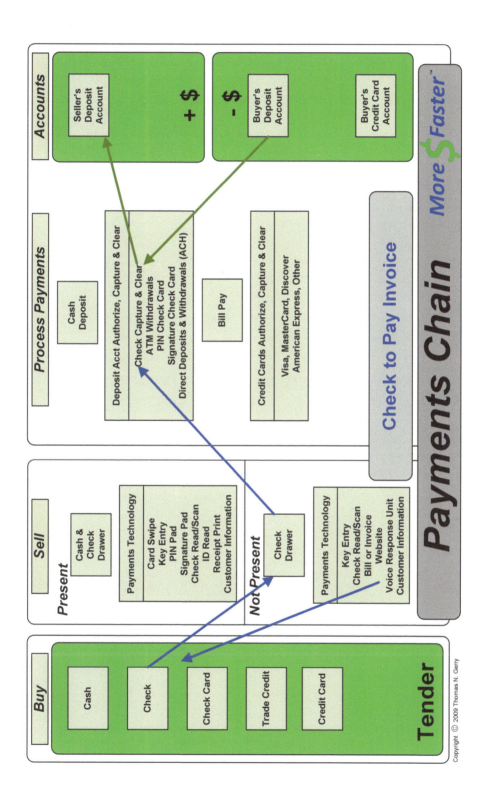

Payments Chain

Buy · Sell · Process Payments · Accounts

Present · Not Present

Check to Pay Invoice

More $ Faster™

Tender

Buy: Cash · Check · Check Card · Trade Credit · Credit Card

Present: Cash & Check Drawer · Payments Technology (Card Swipe, Key Entry, PIN Pad, Signature Pad, Check Read/Scan, ID Read, Receipt Print, Customer Information)

Not Present: Check Drawer · Payments Technology (Key Entry, Check Read/Scan, Bill or Invoice, Website, Voice Response Unit, Customer Information)

Process Payments: Cash Deposit · Deposit Acct Authorize, Capture & Clear (Check Capture & Clear, ATM Withdrawals, PIN Check Card, Signature Check Card, Direct Deposits & Withdrawals (ACH)) · Bill Pay · Credit Cards Authorize, Capture & Clear (Visa, MasterCard, Discover, American Express, Other)

Accounts: Seller's Deposit Account · + $ · − $ · Buyer's Deposit Account · Buyer's Credit Card Account

Out$ - Cards

Purchasing cards are often provided to departments with related budget limits. This works well to streamline processes for miscellaneous expenditures where local decision making is best applied. Just be sure your internal audit has been adapted to ensure good judgment is used with purchasing cards, and misuse or abuse does not generate losses.

If you are considering providing purchasing cards, please research news stories about out-of-control use at universities and government agencies, including personal expenses and spending just to keep from losing discretionary budget levels.

Purchasing cards can easily eliminate many of your internal costs of the traditional purchase order process that ends with payment by checks from invoices received. However, be aware that your suppliers' net usable money can be significantly reduced by their payments costs in accepting and processing purchasing card transactions.

Out$ Card	
Fees	Payment Processing
Expenses	Pre-Approval
	Posting to Expense Accounts
Losses	Unauthorized Purchases

Out$ - "Pal Charges"

If your Internet business payments include PayPal you will want to assess all the fees to make Internet payments. You will find expanded payments chains and more detail in chapter 12.

Out$ – ePay

There are now electronic cash payroll cards and online services for the unbanked, people that do not have deposit accounts at financial institutions, that can improve your profit though lower overall costs.

Out$ ePay	
Fees	Wire Transfer Fees
	Bill Payment Processing
	ACH Origination Transaction Costs
Expenses	Approval
	Review
	File Uploading
Losses	Cost of Security Controls
Delays	Bill Pay - Effective Date Lag

One property management company executive showed me how he processes incoming rental payments, ensures the funds are good, deducts his management percentage and then uploads an ACH origination file to his online banking website. The bank then forwards those ACH direct payments to his property owners' bank accounts.

He knows this is much more effective and less costly than printing and mailing checks like they used to. But, he does not measure the batch and transaction costs buried in the detail of the bank statements. So, it would be hard for him to compare an alternative ACH processor to his bank's service.

Here is a business bill pay problem we heard about from an owner:

Online B2B Bill Pay Story

Business bill pay is offered free by the bank, but operated by a third party. An error in the address of the insurance company resulted in Bart's business insurance policy being inadvertently canceled several times. The bank was not able to get the bill pay servicer to correct this for a number of payment cycles. Bart wasted many hours and suffered growing frustration. His business was at risk during each insurance cancellation period.

If this kind of problem occurs often, the exception costs might be estimated and included in the **Out$** analysis.

Payments and Purchasing Strategy

Knowledge of the costs of your **Out$** choices, and the impact on your suppliers payments costs are both potentially valuable to your enterprise. More and more suppliers expect more electronic forms of payment that can improve their profits.

Some insurance companies require payment by ACH – it is more predictable and produces available funds immediately when posted to their deposit account. They avoid the costs of handling paper checks, too. Just as you are interested in accelerating **In$** by cutting average clearing times while reducing all your payments costs, so are your suppliers. With payments system improvements sometimes both parties may increase profits.

Take Action

Separate and sort **Out$** into three categories of payments out costs – fees, expenses, and losses, and measure delays in payments made.

1. Be sure you understand your bank account charges for checks written, online banking bill payments, direct ACH payments and other services.

2. Document your internal payments controls and processes.

3. Measure your **Out$** lead times and variation.

4. Identify and then focus on most profit potential gain from precision and lower costs.

PART 2

ROLL UP YOUR SLEEVES – INCREASE YOUR PROFITS

Part 1 focused on measurement so you can identify the most profitable improvements and then see how you are doing month by month. First, you determine *What to change*, and now in **Part 2** you will find ideas and guidance on *How to change*.

Experiment and measure - payments will continue to evolve. A method that reduces your payments cost next month may be less effective next year.

Change your policies and procedures. Train and educate your team. Post visual displays of your payments improvement goals and actual results.

Engage with your customers and suppliers. Payments changes that improve your profits may help them too.

More$Faster

www.paymentspower.com

9 IMPROVE *In$*

Now that you know where to focus to improve your profits using **PAYMENTS POWER**, here are tactics, tools and tips to choose from and adapt to your enterprise in stages for *In$*.

Examples of the three strategies of Improve, Switch and Add are given for each type of payments tender:

1. Cash

2. Checks

3. Cards

4. ePayments

Two ACH example payment chains show the possible trade-offs between payments costs and delays—a cost vs. speed worksheet is shown:

1. Telephone eCheck

2. Check Conversion

Two stories illustrate profit improvement opportunities:

1. PIN vs. Signature

2. B2B eCheck

In the next chapter trade credit factoring is explored as a tactic to reduce *F$*, the delays in converting sales into usable money, and dramatically reduce the effect of Days Sales Outstanding (DSO).

9 IMPROVE *In$*

Strategies and Tactics

Following are tactics within the three strategies of Improve, Switch and Add for *In$*. Let's start with innovations and developments in reducing or offsetting the costs of physical cash.

Improve Cash - Currency and Coin

How can you reduce the costs of currency and coin you receive and payout or deposit? The major trends are cash back, and currency and coin management outsourcing.

In$ Cash	
Improve	Cash back on PIN Debit can reduce daily currency and coin inventory and associated costs.
Switch	Cash management outsourcing - smart vaults can provide same day usable funds and eliminate the burden and risk of transporting cash deposits to the bank.
Add	Add lobby kiosk ATM

Another affordable cash technology is the lobby kiosk ATM. Refurbished units are available for less than $2,000 for the DIY business person. Aside from reducing payments risk from check or card payments, the ATM can also generate fee income for the store to help offset cash payments costs.

There are services available which do not require a capital purchase of the ATM, with a smaller portion of revenue share.

Think of the captive ATM as a currency recycle technology - your customers and your employees can withdraw cash for their use without going to the bank or supermarket - some of the sales cash you received.

In$ Card	
Improve	Request Interchange Cost Plus from your merchant services supplier. Identify and fix downgrade causes like missing address verification data, CVVS codes, or key entry instead of swipe read. Add Level 3 invoice and order data to business card account payments.
Switch	Change from your current merchant services supplier to one that offers Interchange Cost Plus processing and reporting. If your average check card transactions exceed $20, and your customers can use a PIN pad when paying, shift your card transaction mix from signature to PIN debit through training and customer communication. Encourage payment by check instead of the more expensive card types.
Add	Self-service ACH origination to avoid costs and delays in accepting checks Your own non-monetary rewards programs for more profitable payments types

Improve Credit Card Payments

Knowledge is power—first you have to see exactly how your credit card transactions are classified for purposes of assessing interchange and processing charges. You will want transparency in all statements from the Payments Chain steps; card authorizations and settlement, gateway charges, even the last step - deposits to your bank account.

Improve or Switch to Interchange Cost Plus

Request that your merchant services processing and billing be changed to *Interchange Cost Plus*. Once that is completed check the next monthly statements to be sure you can see standard interchange classification counts, totals and processing costs. The monthly statements and online reporting should allow you to separate the pass-through association and network mandated costs, and the interchange charges, from the authorization, capture, settlement and processing costs.

If that vendor or bank does not or will not switch you to interchange cost plus, or provide easy to understand reporting, you should find a processor that does offer this newer, much more transparent approach.

You may already be enjoying *Cost Plus* pricing. However, many enterprises still have not discovered the profit revealing opportunity in completely transparent, detailed statements that show the transactions labeled with association standard classification descriptions and every processing charge.

This option in credit card processing used to be just for higher volume merchants that have the knowledge and the leverage to negotiate a cost plus processing agreement. When MasterCard and Visa made public the details of their hundreds of interchange classifications in recent years, this option became more well-known and desirable. If you have a processor contract that is priced with a simple bundled cost, you are likely to find this a valuable chance to improve your profit opportunity by changing to interchange cost plus.

If you are used to the categories of qualified, mid-, and non-qualified on your statements you may want to invest in a deeper understanding of your credit card payments. By improving your processing arrangement to *Interchange Cost Plus* you should receive statement data you can use for analysis of your payments operations, to understand your real payments costs for forecasting, and to uncover specific improvement opportunities.

Anti-trust Justice Department Action

October 2010 a civil lawsuit was filed against rules that American Express, MasterCard and Visa apply to stop merchants from offering their customers discounts and rewards and information about card

---

B2B/G Tip

   If you are selling business–to-business or business-to-government, perhaps accepting payments with purchasing cards, be sure to find out if you are including required Level 2 or 3 invoice and order data.

   If not, you could be leaving as much as 100 basis points of those sales dollars on the table.

---

costs. American Express is fighting the suit, the other two card associations settled. This is another big opening for experimentation to improve your profits.

Switch from Signature Debit to PIN Debit to Reduce Interchange

During one of my workshops when Susan, the checkout clerk, saw the payments worksheet with a goal of 90% PIN vs. Signature debit transactions, she immediately voiced her doubt. She said that the customers that used their major bank check cards always insisted on signing instead of entering their PIN. They believe the rewards points they earn by signing are very valuable. Their checking statement inserts remind them regularly to use "Credit" (signature) instead of entering their PIN.

Susan's customers do not know how much that choice costs the business. We talked about the speed and security benefits for customers entering their PIN, and placement of the PIN pad on the counter.

Strive to understand your customers' payments behaviors and preferences to harvest more profit. Your customers are the ultimate test and judge of changes and payments experiments and procedures you try.

Several checkout people have told me they do not encourage their customers to use the PIN pad. They thought PIN transactions were more costly. These cases are evidence of poor understanding of payments costs.

If the transaction is over $15 to $20, PIN debit payments are likely to incur less total payment cost. As the average transaction amount exceeds that range, the payments cost advantage for PIN grows dramatically. PIN based ATM network charges are typically lower than credit/ signature based interchange for larger payment amounts.

Studies have shown buyers prefer PIN over Signature Debit. Because issuing banks receive more interchange income from signature than PIN debit, most financial institutions try to influence payment behavior by either rewarding the use of signature or penalizing customers by charging extra fees for PIN transactions. The figure below highlights this conflict:

Debit Card Profit Conflict	Sign	PIN
Card Association	✓	
Issuing Bank/CU	✓	
Consumer		✓
Enterprise		✓

So, when you can, you should make it easy and encourage your customers to use the PIN pad. You also want to encourage them to use their check card instead of a credit card whenever possible to reduce your payments costs.

The Federal Reserve issued their proposed regulations on debit card interchange and routing for comment in December, 2010. When the regulations are issued in April, 2011, the dynamics of debit card payments costs may be very different than now.

The changes in debit card regulations are an important reason you should begin using the **PAYMENTS POWER** framework and measurements. If you do not track how your payments processor is applying the regulation changes, you may lose some profit.

PIN vs. Signature Story

Like most retail service businesses, RepairStar is experiencing a growing portion of check card payments. However their PIN debit transactions were only 0.3% of revenue, with signature debit at 19%. Other retail stores have a mix of 3:2 or even as high as 7:1 of PIN over signature.

This is important, because with debit card average transaction amounts over $100, this business can improve profits by reducing cost over 1% on almost 20% of their revenue. This is equivalent of saving 20 basis points on total sales. At $2 million sales annually, this improvement alone is worth $4,000.

Implementation required education of checkout cashiers and proper placement of the PIN pad for maximum customer convenience and security. A simple visual display posted on the bulletin board in the team break area shows monthly improvement in the mix of check card payments, PIN vs. signature, and resulting payments cost savings—a higher *M$*.

Switch from Credit Card to ACH to Eliminate Interchange

In an earlier example I noted that a single high dollar credit card transaction can cost hundreds of dollars in interchange. If the customer is willing to pay in advance when making the charter reservation with an electronic check, an ACH entry, the charter company profits can increase by hundreds of dollars. The transaction can be done by phone, by e-mail, by fax or through a secure website eCheck.

Note that credit card association rules typically prohibit charging buyers a premium for use of credit cards, but allow discounts for cash or other payment means. Those rules are under attack.

There are different regulations, rules, laws and legal case precedents for ACH versus credit cards though, so be sure you understand the different risks and operational requirements before changing some card payments to ACH.

The latest ACH technologies support two innovations- *Business self-service* and *End Customer self-service*. Comprehensive risk management is also becoming available for ACH, and you should understand and control the different risks of ACH payments, for **In$** and **Out$**.

Secure Vault

Secure Vault is a unique ACH based payments approach just recently out of an extended pilot program that some banks are offering their enterprise customers. Buyers can choose to make payments on a commercial website and then are automatically sent to their own bank's online banking for authentication where they select which account they wish to pay from. Then they link back to the original website to get a payment confirmation. There is no need to provide any bank account information to the seller or biller.

This is currently one of the only online ACH transactions payment programs with real-time authorization and guaranteed payments. Although the processing and settlement costs are higher than offline ACH, the costs are lower than credit card and some debit card processing and interchange.

The Secure Vault service is not available at every financial institution yet, but you should be aware of innovations coming on-stream built on the low cost ACH electronic payments foundation.

In$ — ACH Payment Chain Example

Once a credit or debit card online authorization is received, transaction return item risk of insufficient available credit for businesses and card processors is virtually eliminated. ACH withdrawals from checking and savings accounts are different. ACH return item risk management is usually achieved by withdrawing funds from the paying account and waiting until a return is unlikely before sending the ACH deposit to the receiving account.

ACH processors can set the number of business days from the day of sending the withdrawal transaction before the deposit transaction is submitted for posting to allow time for possible returns and an opportunity to communicate and resolve any rejected withdrawal transaction. Based on risk and processing fees, the number of days can range from zero to more than five. The lowest cost ACH processing may have the longest delays from the withdrawal to the deposit.

At the other extreme, you can get same day credit on a telephone eCheck if you submit by 10:00 am, but the cost is nearly 3% of the transactions amount. Here is a step by step story and a payment chain diagram example illustrating a common ACH process and lag time scenario.

Telephone Payment by Customer
Karen answers the phone at the vet clinic

Step 1: Monday 10:00 am—the customer calls to make a boarding reservation for her pet and elects to pay the first night from a checking account instead of a credit card. Karen enters the transaction in the web-based ACH application.

Step 2: Monday by 3:00 pm-Karen submits the ACH batch including the telephone payment. The ACH processor sends an ACH withdrawal transaction through the clearing system

Step 3: Tuesday—the ACH Processor receives the withdrawn money from the customer's checking account.

Step 4: Wednesday for Thursday availability—the processor sends the ACH deposit transaction through the clearing system to be posted by the Vet Clinic's bank so the money is in their checking account Thursday morning.

Funds are available in the clinic's checking account *three business days* after the customer pays.

Discussions on improving the speed of ACH clearing and settlement have been ongoing for years. A phrase, *Same Day Settlement*, captures the spirit of this topic.

There is great opportunity for innovation in B2B payments, but there seems to be more attention on consumer payments concerns. Major opportunities to improve payments for sellers remain for real innovators. After all, why can't an all electronic ACH transaction clear as fast as or faster than a scanned paper check? And at much less cost, since the cost of sending the check front and back images is eliminated.

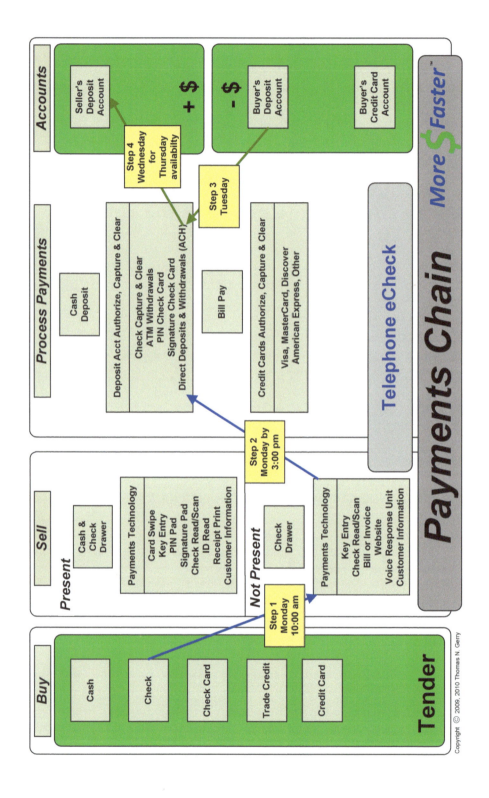

If you can get one day or two day availability on checks deposited, why can you not get the same or faster on ACH transactions submitted?

In$ Check	
Improve	Integrate eCheck payments (ACH) into point of sale applications, collections systems, accounts receivables systems, customer relationship management (CRM) or accounting applications
Switch	Credit and debit cards to electronic checks
Add	Self-service web-based ACH for one time and recurring payments eCheck payment on your website

Some banks offer comparable availability on ACH as on check deposits. Does yours? Check your deposit dates against the dates your funds are made available. There are still many business customers that report delays, *F$,* longer than one or two days even on check deposits. This will be more important to you if interest rates rise in coming years as many experts predict.

Storage Unit Monthly Rent

Another example is storage unit monthly rental payments. The best ACH processing can automatically originate any recurring payment on any frequency for any contract period. Some offer integration to storage unit application software to eliminate any redundant input.

As an alternative to a storage unit renter paying by mailing a paper check every month, the management can rent the unit and obtain permission to automatically withdraw the payments from a checking account. This can be done one or two days in advance of the due date by explaining that the storage company will be paid on the due date with collected funds so late fees can be prevented. All the disclosures can be on the recurring payment section of the rental agreement.

This is also a great alternative to a recurring customer credit card not present payment—a profit improvement of about 2% of revenue.

ACH Cost vs. Speed Trade-off

If the delays in these examples are too long for your business to accept, you may want to find an ACH processor that offers you faster availability, even at a higher cost or with reserve options or premiums to offset return item risk.

The following figure illustrates this trade off and representative *M$* you might find with four day versus same day deposits to your bank account.

ACH Choices *In$*	F$	M$
More Usable $	4 days	$ 99.00
	3 days	$ 98.50
	2 days	$ 98.00
	1 day	$ 97.50
Get $ Faster	0 day	$ 97.00

ACH 1.0, 1.5 and 2.0 generations

ACH 1.0 is traditional file upload to your bank for origination. This path can produce a low per transaction cost, but the trade-off is lack of integration, with higher manual costs. Another cost is potentially higher risk of returns handling. ACH 2.0 is web-based front-end processing, risk management and file and exceptions handling which can lower overall costs even though the total per transaction service charges may be higher. Online business banking ACH origination is somewhere in the middle - perhaps we should think of that as ACH 1.5.

Which is right for you? ACH 1.0, 1.5 or 2.0? The answer starts with understanding the pros and cons of the alternatives and then estimating and measuring the costs and speed when used in your payments environment.

Improve-Integrate Point of Sale, Lockbox and Website Checkout

There are many vertical market applications that offer integrated credit and debit card processing. Voice response systems today often can accept telephone payments using checking accounts. Adding eChecks to your Internet checkout can save payments costs and even increase sales by adding another customer payment choice beyond just credit cards and PayPal.

Ask if the software is open through APIs, application programming interfaces, to further payments integration.

Today you can utilize bank or self-service lockbox capabilities which capture remittance information as well as the payments images and data for complete integration with accounts receivable and general accounting applications. The more advanced lockbox capabilities also handle other payment types in addition to checks. If your incoming mail check volumes are substantial, you may find profit through integrating a lockbox service.

Add Electronic Deposit of Checks Received

In financial institutions two technologies, branch capture, and ATMs with check deposit imaging have virtually eliminated daily courier costs from branches to a central check processing facility.

This has allowed many banks and credit unions to extend the daily deadline for accepting same day deposits—a competitive advantage over those institutions that continue to transport checks deposited by customers.

The technology has been extended to business checking customers' locations to also eliminate their transportation costs, delays and risks.

This payments innovation driven by the national law commonly known as Check 21 which was passed after 9/11 (aircraft carrying checks for clearing sat on the ground for many days after the attacks), promises faster availability of funds with end to end electronic clearing.

It can also give you faster knowledge of insufficient funds.

Finally, let's look at two more variations.

Switch from Checks to ACH

Both front office and back office check conversion to ACH can bring payments costs down. A new generation of desktop deposit can automatically select the most cost effective and compliant payments chain path – either ACH or Check 21. Some paper checks cannot be converted to ACH. For those you need Check 21 eDeposit. The Electronic Payments Association NACHA rules define the qualification conditions.

Improve NSF Checks Collection—Reduce Losses and Collection Costs from NSF Checks Received for In$

Within the next few years many checks that are returned for insufficient or uncollected funds, NSF checks, originally deposited by business (whether they come back in paper or image or ACH form) will be collected with an ACH process instead of simply being re-deposited or collected by phone and mail. A special ACH transaction type was added several years ago for this purpose. This is called RCK, for returned check transactions.

This approach may not cost the business depositor any processing fees, but can eliminate substantial internal work, and the processor and perhaps the financial institution are compensated for the work. How is that possible? First, at the point of sale or in your statements you must notify the buyers of this electronic re-presentment and an additional collection charge if their checks are returned NSF.

The person who writes the check pays for this. All the processing and electronic collection costs are covered by state allowable fees that are also drafted or electronically withdrawn from the NSF check writer's account.

Some studies indicate the national averages of traditional collection of NSF checks is about 45% effective and the funds delay can be over 30 days from when the check was written. The ACH method can improve that to 80% to 85% effective, 100% of the check face amount, received within seven to fifteen days.

How does ACH RCK accomplish these powerful results?

1. Intelligent re-presentment—the technology submits on days that are likely to be paydays or direct deposits days for benefits.

2. ACH RCK is allowed two re-presentments vs. only one time for re-deposited checks or check image transactions.

3. ACH RCK transactions enjoy priority of posting before other checks that may also be clearing that day, so the likelihood of the ACH item successfully posting is higher.

What about the 15% of NSF checks not collected electronically? Secondary collection companies, when successful, can deliver maybe as much as 70% of face value of any revenue recovered. The discount pays for their services.

Put eCheck Payment Options on Your Website

Let your customers enter their checking routing transit and account number to make a payment to you. This will cost you much less than handling a paper check, or suffering the cost of credit card interchange and processing.

You may notice in your internet shopping that many sites now present the e-check payments windows before ever showing the credit card or PayPal options. Why? Because the ACH transaction costs are usually much lower. You can measure if ACH returns are higher than card chargebacks for your web sales.

ACH Returns Trade-offs

Include the returns volumes and fees in your costs analysis. Here's an example provided by an excellent ACH processor. If a client normally experiences a significant return rate, then the returns processing fees can be more important than the per item processing charge. A $0.20 per item processing cost plus a return item fee of $5.00 is effectively $0.70 per item at a 10% return rate, while a seemingly more expensive processor offer of $0.30 per transaction with a return fee of $3.00 is really only effectively $0.60 per transaction.

In$ ePay	
Improve	Request that ACH incoming payments include invoice ID and line numbers.
Switch	Encourage customers to pay through eCheck on your website.
Add	Self-service web-based ACH for one time and recurring payments. Electronic invoicing and payment service.

Use an electronic Invoice and Payment Service

There are now very powerful ACH-based online services that let you send electronic invoices which your customers can review and authorize payment against, even down to the line item level. This eliminates most of the costs and delays of the old paper-based process. It also takes away the excuse of not paying an entire invoice just because of a problem with one of the line items. The best systems support payments against multiple outstanding invoices, too.

The following story illustrates use of currently available technology to improve cost and speed, without forcing significant investment on customers to take advantage of the improvements. In fact, the changes often will lead to improvements in customer accounts payable processes too.

This story is playing out across the US, in all types and sizes of enterprises for B2B sales. The real barrier is the attitude, "If it isn't broke, don't fix it!" On the other hand, a continuous improvement culture will drive this kind of profit improvement.

B2B eCheck Story

Great Northern trucking delivery customers pay by paper check from invoices like most business-to-business payments. However some of them are sending checks just from delivery tickets, not waiting for invoices. The high volume of checks received result in several trips to the bank daily.

Some are even requesting to pay by ACH, to improve their own payables processes.

By switching from paper checks, Great Northern can accelerate receipts—especially if they can convince customers to pay by website eCheck based on delivery tickets, or electronic invoices.

The cost savings are dramatic for both the payer and payee. The trucking company eliminates invoice preparation and mailing costs, and the work to prepare and transport paper checks deposits to the bank.

Receivables are collected many days faster by cutting the time lag delays from delivery date to invoice to check receipt to collected funds in the bank.

Their customers save costs of their preparation and mailing of paper checks, yet have no capital investment. They just login to the trucking company website to make the payments online.

Trade Credit Factoring

Next let's go to a separate chapter for the last tactic. If you do not offer B2B Trade Credit to your buyers, just skip the next chapter.

Take Action

Choose and implement tactics to improve *In$* performance of both *M$* and *F$*. Learn about and choose a mix of ACH 1.0, 1.5 and 2.0 capabilities to fit your needs.

1. Currency and Coin - Add kiosk ATMs, encourage PIN Debit cash back.

2. Cards – Reduce processing costs first with transparency to measure and manage transactions - Interchange Cost Plus.

3. Cards – Switch to other payments technology to eliminate interchange.

4. Checks - Eliminate paper with check imaging electronic deposit (Check 21).

5. Checks - Add point of sale, lockbox or website integrated eCheck capability.

6. NSF Checks - Collect all insufficient funds returns electronically with ACH.

7. Add electronic invoicing with ACH payments built-in.

10 Improve B2B Trade Credit *In$*

If your enterprise offers Trade Credit to buyers, you are interested in reducing Days Sales Outstanding and *F$*. This chapter is about Factoring.

Factoring adds an intermediate step to Trade Credit and changes the final step. This addition, step 2, and changes to step 3, are detailed in this chapter:

1. Sale Day—the buyer acquires the goods and services for a promise to pay.

2. A few days later—the seller gets usable funds in exchange for the Accounts Receivable asset.

3. 30, 60, 90 days or more later—the factor is repaid from usable funds from the buyer, and the costs of factoring for the seller are finalized and collected.

Innovations are emerging in Factoring:

- Broader availability at lower cost—not just for the Fortune 500

- Related services including credit underwriting and collections

Factoring may be a powerful tool in your journey to improve *F$,* even if your *M$* decreases. Overall, in some businesses it may be worth accelerating cash flow, even if payments costs increase. The secret is you might then offer much more attractive payments terms to dramatically increase your competitive advantage.

10 IMPROVE B2B TRADE CREDIT *In$*

As a seller of products and services to businesses and governments, a B2B/G enterprise most likely offers trade credit terms. At the moment of a sale, instead of collecting a check, card or electronic payment from the buyer, the seller creates an accounts receivable asset, a loan to the buyer that will be repaid after 30, 60, 90 or more days. Most B2B companies have their own credit decision, invoicing and collection processes. Extending Trade credit is another line of business completely different than the core competency of the enterprise, but usually a necessary practice in an industry or line of business.

Instead of usable money, trade credit produces, at least in the short term, an inventory of promises to pay. Factoring exchanges that inventory of payment promises for usable money, at a discount and with various costs. Factoring improves *F$*, but reduces *M$*.

A Similar Practice in Residential Lending

In financial institutions it is normal to consider credits or loans as products, which, even before the loans are originated, may be created for resale to a secondary market that demands certain types of investments. The financial institutions earn their value through origination fees and servicing charges that continue after the loan is sold, and the secondary market buyer as the ultimate owner of the loan asset earns the interest over the life of the loan.

The customer relationship and the loan servicing often remain between a mortgage originating financial institution and the borrower, even as the ultimate purchaser of the loan may be anywhere in the world.

Some B2B enterprises are able to sell their trade credit assets to a factor to get usable funds from their sales in just a few days instead of 30, 60 or 90+ days. B2B Accounts Receivable Factoring is a special kind of secondary market.

Factoring Steps

Factoring extends the trade credit from the two steps identified in Chapter 7 to three. It adds costs the seller pays the factor, but can let the seller offer even longer terms to buyers for competitive advantage while at the same time reducing the delay in converting sales into usable money to just days. If the costs are right, factoring can improve profits and support growth while shrinking accounts payable Days Sales Outstanding (DSO) dramatically.

However, most small to medium businesses have had less than ideal alternatives. An emerging innovation may be worth your review. But first is a review of how factoring works. For a clear understanding of the impacts on *M$* and *F$*, let's look at what happens in all three steps.

Step	Buyer Purchase		
		Debit	**Credit**
First	**Buyer**	**Expense or Asset**	**Accounts Payable**
		Debit	**Credit**
Sale Day	**Seller**	**Accounts Receivable**	**Revenue**

The first step, on the day of the sale, is the same as in the traditional trade credit process. Instead of tendering cash, check, credit card or electronic payment, the buyer creates an obligation to pay in the future, the accounts payable credit that matches the purchase, which might be an expense or an asset, a debit.

Instead of money the seller creates an asset, a debit to accounts receivable that will result in an invoice or request for buyer payment in the future. The seller generates revenue, a credit, in this step. But not cash flow!

The second step is to sell the buyer obligation to pay in the future to the factor. This can be pre-arranged and underwritten so the non-cash accounts receivable asset can be quickly converted into usable funds in the seller's bank account.

Step	Factor Buys A/R		
Second **Two to** **Three** **Days** **Later**	Factor	**Debit**	**Credit**
		Accounts Receivable	Cash
		Fee Cash	Revenue
	Seller	**Debit**	**Credit**
		Cash	Accounts Receivable
		Expense	Fee Cash

There are innovative true factoring services coming to market that utilize web-based technology for speed and lower cost than the legacy alternatives. If you are interested in more information, go to the website www.paymentspower.com or e-mail me, tomgerry@paymentspower.com.

I suggest you consider the fees and interest you pay a factor to be part of your payments cost for the tender of trade credit.

Finally, the third step shown on the next page happens many days later – the buyer pays with a money tender, usually by business check. This payment repays the factor and clears that accounts receivable. Because the buyer controls the timing of the payment, it is only upon collecting that money the factor can determine the total interest carrying costs and final fees, all paid by the seller.

There is a payments system improvement opportunity in this step to replace the paper checks with ACH transactions as described earlier in this book.

The best of true factoring includes a menu of related outsourcing services—the credit underwriting, ongoing credit monitoring, and collections processes. This outsourcing to a niche business with core competence in trade credit lending may reduce your internal costs to partially offset the factoring external fees and interest. You will be able to focus on your core competency. In addition to gaining the major portion of sales money in just days, you can proactively offer even longer trade credit terms.

Step	Buyer Payment		
Third **30, 60, 90 + Days Later**	Buyer	Debit	Credit
		Accounts Payable	Cash
	Factor	Debit	Credit
		Cash	Accounts Receivable
		Fee Cash	Revenue
	Seller	Expense	Fee Cash

Look at all three steps to assess the trade-off between increasing payments costs, therefore reducing *M$*, and significantly reducing the delay of usable money in your bank accounts, *F$.*

Take Action

Choose and implement tactics to improve Trade Credit *In$* performance of *F$*, even if *M$* is reduced.

Research web based Factoring innovations for competitive advantage and cash flow.

1. Easy and fast *F$* reduction

2. Outsource credit underwriting and collections to offset Factoring fees

3. Offer even longer payment terms to win sales, even as you improve your cash flow

11 IMPROVE *Out$*

Now that you know where to focus to improve your profits using **PAYMENTS POWER** with payments received, here are tactics, tools and tips to choose from and adapt to your enterprise in stages for *Out$*.

Because Checks are still the primary payment tender for businesses this chapter covers improvements in check payments and related electronic payments.

Two alternatives for ACH processing are clarified and electronic invoicing is compared:

- Direct Deposit

- Direct Withdrawal

Two ACH example payment chains show the possible trade-offs between payments costs and delays:

1. Direct deposit of net pay

2. Web ACH *Out$*

Two stories illustrate profit improvement opportunities:

1. B2B Bill Pay

2. B2B Checks

11 IMPROVE *Out$*

Now let's examine the three strategies of Improve, Switch and Add for payments to suppliers and employees. Because studies indicate that up to 85% of business payments are still by paper check, this chapter will focus on several available methods used today. This table summarizes a few tactics to improve profits from actively changing your payments out, *Out$*.

Out$ Check	
Improve	Eliminate any payroll checks for un-banked employees with reusable stored value payroll cards (see paymentspower.com for details). Provide an in-house ATM kiosk for your employees convenience to get cash from their stored value payroll cards.
Switch	If a supply partner offers eInvoice, change your accounts payable process to utilize this instead of paper checks.
Add	Use self-service Web ACH Origination - Pay supply chain partners and reimburse employees electronically. Use Purchasing card accounts for discretionary departmental expenditures.

A surprising number of working people do not have financial institution deposit accounts. For them a payroll direct deposit is impossible. A paper check must be cashed to become usable money. Aside from the risks of theft and just losing folding money, cashing payroll checks and buying money orders incur fees that reduce the person's usable wages. Stored value payroll cards can be used at stores for purchases and cash back, and at ATMs.

Switch – eInvoice

Your suppliers may be improving their payments systems just as you are. You may be asked to pay from electronic invoices instead of paper. The best of this technology allows you to upload payments approval data for invoices, even at the line item level if you do not wish to pay an entire invoice. There are third party technology and processing costs, but the benefits of eliminating paper invoices and paper checks can be significant for you and your suppliers.

Add – Web ACH Direct Withdrawal and Deposit

There are several electronic *Out$* methods. To reduce confusion I will not use the terms ACH Debit and ACH Credit. Rather, let's identify deposits that increase usable balances and withdrawals that decrease account balances. This table summarizes three ACH *Out$* variations.

Choices	Pro	Con
Web ACH Direct Deposit	Buyer initiates and controls timing precisely to send payment to Seller; no interchange, lowest payments cost	Seller has to allow Buyer to directly deposit payment to Seller's deposit account; Buyer may neglect to enter data to relate payment to the invoice or line items
Web ACH Direct Withdrawal	Seller initiates and collects money directly after Buyer authorization; no interchange, lowest payments cost	Buyer has to allow Seller to directly withdraw money from buyer's deposit account
Electronic Invoice & Approval	Neither party discloses deposit account numbers except to 3rd party. Accounts Payable uploads line item OK, ACH transactions post, and Accounts Receivable downloads what was paid	Added payments costs for third party to send eInvoice and originate Buyer ACH withdrawal and Seller ACH deposit 24

All three methods can eliminate cost and delays of paper checks. One business owner asked why he should want to give up the check float, the time from when his bookkeeper writes checks until they finally clear their checking account. Here is the answer – more predictable cash management – with Web ACH payments, his bookkeeper can wait longer to pay and know more precisely when the transactions will clear.

ACH Risk and Settlement Delay

As described in an earlier chapter, ACH Withdrawals from checking and savings accounts are more like paper checks than card purchase transactions. ACH processors manage their return item risk by withdrawing funds from your bank account before depositing funds to your suppliers' or employees' accounts. ACH processors set the number of business days from the day of sending the withdrawal transaction before the deposit transaction is sent for posting to allow time for a rejected withdrawal to happen and then to communicate and resolve the situation with you.

Based on risk and processing fees, the number of days can range from zero to more than five. The following written example and payments chain diagram represents only one possible scenario. The lowest cost ACH processing may have the longest delay from the withdrawal to the deposit.

Replace Paper Paychecks with ACH Direct Deposit

Step 1 Monday Morning—The administrator completes the Quick-Books payroll calculations and enters the net pay transactions into the web-based ACH application.

Step 2 Monday by 3:00 pm—after balancing and approval the batch is submitted to the ACH processor. The withdrawal is sent through the ACH clearing system to the business's bank.

Step 3 Wednesday or Thursday Morning –If the withdrawal has been rejected for any reason the ACH processor contacts the business to resolve the issue.

Step 4 Thursday—The ACH processor sends the pay deposit transactions through the clearing system to all your employees' different banks for each financial institution to post in their end of day batch processing Thursday night or early Friday morning. Employees and their family members can make ATM withdrawals or pay bills without the need to physically take a paper payroll check to the bank to deposit or cash.

Payday Friday—The employees receive QuickBooks paystubs instead of paychecks.

The employees have available funds in their checking accounts **at the time of posting at the end of three business days or early the forth business day** counting from the day the pay deposit batch is submitted.

By sending the pay deposit transactions on Thursday for a Friday payday the ACH processor ensures the funds are available for ATM and teller withdrawals even at the start of payday.

Because payroll is one of the biggest and most critical recurring payments events, this ACH processor requires submission an additional day early, on Monday for a Friday payday, to have time to deal with any other variation in the payments chain that might cause a day delay to the pay deposit transactions. Of course, we all know that employees rely absolutely on being paid on the expected payday.

For example, if a bookkeeping error caused a bank balance to be insufficient to cover all the pay deposits scheduled for Friday, the ACH processor can call Wednesday or Thursday to resolve the issue during that day so the employees will be paid Friday.

The simple truth is the most effective risk management in ACH processing today is to submit a withdrawal, wait a day or two to be sure the withdrawal is not returned, and then once the processor is sure they have collected funds, make the associated deposit or deposits.

That is what this payroll example illustrates - a single withdrawal from the business's bank account, receipt of the funds into the processor's bank account, and finally the deposits sent to the individual employee's financial institutions.

Here is the Payments Chain to show these steps and delays graphically.

The payment chain diagram headings are different in this payments example because the Employer is paying for work performed by the employees and starting all the payments processing that ends in direct deposits into the employee's bank accounts, or perhaps in stored value payroll cards, kind of an extended personal bank.

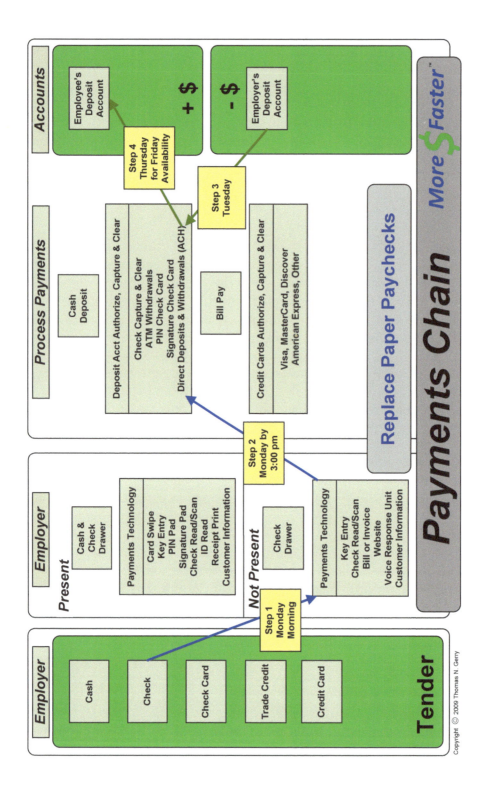

There are trade-offs in payments cost vs. speed because of the offline, batch nature of ACH. ACH does not protect the seller or the payments processor with a point of sales online authorization or hold against the paying account like a card transaction does.

However, this is changing. The Visa POS Check Service may be another variation of real-time authorizations against live bank accounts. Today this is just for paper check conversions and only with limited participating banks, just a hint of the future.

Why not use an online business bill payment service? Web ACH gives more precise, tighter control of the effective payment date. Instead of using a bill payment that may have a required delay of three to five business days, you can originate ACH payments that will clear in one to two days. There are some ACH processors that will take on risk from reducing the days of delay, for a price, naturally. This figure illustrates speed vs. cost alternatives, though the **L$** you may find are likely to be different than shown here.

ACH Choices *Out$*	F$	L$
Less Pmt Cost $	4 days	$ 101.00
	3 days	$ 101.80
	2 days	$ 102.50
	1 day	$ 103.00
Keep $ Longer	0 day	$ 104.00

ACH can be a self-service web-based bill payment, maybe better in some ways than online bill pay services. You set up your supplier's bank routing and transit number and checking account number instead of having a 3rd party bill payment company do that. You can also set up recurring payments and directly control their frequency, timing and amounts. So, I recommend you consider the alternative to pay suppliers direct instead of with paper checks or online bill pay for much more predictable cash management.

For example—pay exactly the latest day to earn a timely payment discount and eliminate the uncertainty of mail or weather delays in transit.

Online B2B Bill Pay Story

In an earlier story Andy was unhappy with the five business day lead time to make an online bill payment—longer than delivery of a check by mail locally.

By switching to self-service ACH payment origination, the restaurant owner Andy keeps the freedom of making payments anytime, anywhere, but he can initiate the payment as late as 48 to 72 hours in advance of the due date. So, he can be sure the payment is not later than required, but also no earlier than needed. He has choices, too. He can have a tighter lead time, say 24 to 48 hours, at a higher processing cost.

Self-service ACH does cost Andy more than the free Business Bill Pay offered by his bank, but he can manage cash payments, *Out$*, much more precisely – 2-3 days vs. 5-10 days from payment to receipt by his suppliers.

Expense Reimbursement Comparison

Even if you are using payroll direct deposit, you may still be printing paper checks for employee travel reimbursements. There is an easy to understand visual process example on the website of switching from paper checks to direct ACH payment for expense reimbursements. You can download two process flowcharts to compare the differences.

The process flowchart has been shown to be a powerful tool to visualize all the steps and all the internal and external people and departments that have to be involved. Identifying the steps and the players will help you discover all the delays and waste, and costs for your payments measurement framework.

The following benefits are shown with these flowcharts:

- Go Green - Eliminate transport and delivery for branch deposit; no paper, ink, envelope or stamp required

- Faster and lowest cost – five process steps eliminated, up to four days quicker reimbursement.

Following this B2B Checks story is a simple payments chain diagram for a self-service Web ACH buyer originated transaction. Notice how few steps are required. In supply chain terms, this can simplify and reduce variability in *cash to cash* measurements.

B2B Checks Story

The founding patriarch is still active in the business; one son is President, and another Chief Operating Officer. Checks are printed enough in advance so the founder can look at them and they can be mailed five days before due.

Switching to self-service ACH origination for all outgoing payments offers surprising benefits, including a superior way for the patriarch to review each payment. With online access anywhere, anytime up to batch release point he has a 'Just in Time, Up to the last minute' control to review and hold any individual disbursement.. He does not have to come to the office as he does with physical checks. Mr. Dave can spend more time at the cabin.

With direct ACH payments instead of sending checks five days in advance of when due, the controller can wait until just two days before, and the payments batch details are accessible online with the proper security.

For their supply chain partners the benefits are significant too. Payments are never late from the trucking company; collected funds are direct deposited, paper checks deposits are eliminated along with the delay for the checks to clear.

This story brings out some of the hidden benefits brought by web based payments innovations - review and decide anywhere, anytime.

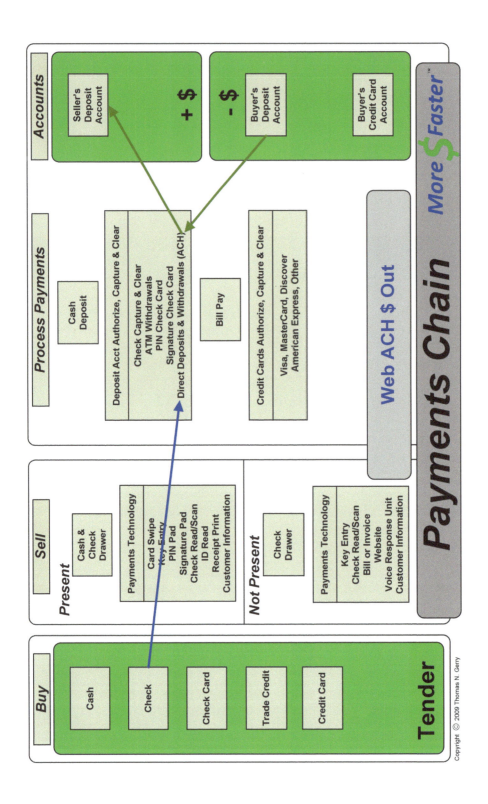

There is natural resistance to change, but around the world enterprises have found that ongoing improvement is key to remaining competitive and profitable.

PAYMENTS POWER supports continual improvement. The measurement framework lets you document and assess the current situation, design the future, and then count and communicate the profit increase.

Take Action

Currently up to 85% of business payments are by check; move to some form of electronic payment to reduce costs or increase speed and precision of *Out$*.

1. Evaluate *L$* and *F$* trade-offs with payment chains

2. If payroll is still by check, consider ACH direct or payroll services

3. Choose Bank Bill Payment, or ACH direct, or Purchasing Cards as needed for different categories of *Out$* to lower *L$* and optimize *F$*

More$Faster

www.paymentspower.com

12 Learn Internet Payments and PayPal™

For eCommerce, this chapter includes more information on Gateways and PayPal.

The two payments chain templates are modified to add PayPal services:

1. Simple payments chain with PayPal high-level components

2. *Behind the curtain* payments chain with extensive PayPal capabilities

Recent changes opening the PayPal application programming interfaces and services to solution developers are summarized.

A modest view into the Internet "crystal ball" is offered to spark your own vision and speculation.

If you are just starting in eCommerce, I recommend you buy the book *Selling Online 2.0*. Author Michael Miller presents a complete picture including insights and comparisons on PayPal competition from Amazon, Google, Yahoo and other emerging payments approaches appropriate for sales volumes below the thresholds where full merchant services processing solutions are needed.

Just a few days ago I used the Moneybookers and Share*It! Alternatives for online buying. By the time you read these words those may be gone, but replaced by several other online payments choices.

12 LEARN INTERNET PAYMENTS AND PAYPAL™

Internet credit card and check card payments are *Card not present* so risk of fraud and chargebacks is higher for sellers. For buyers there is a risk of hackers intercepting and stealing card information. Though not the only way for crooks to get sensitive payments data, internet hacking has been a perceived barrier to internet shopping.

PayPal and others appeared to meet this perceived need for security of buyer information, and certainty of payments for internet sellers.

Gateways

When Internet commerce began, a new type of authorization and capture interface was developed. Authorization and capture services that connect through programming interfaces to web sites are commonly called Gateways.

In addition to website checkouts, Gateway authorization and capture is often found integrated with brick and mortar software applications such as veterinary and restaurant systems.

Gateway technology has also evolved into virtual terminals which are simply online PCs with payments components added such as plastic card readers, PIN key pads and electronic signature pads, even check scanners. These have replaced the separate card swipe terminal devices in some locations.

eCommerce Gateways

There are many choices to implement eCommerce payments. Shopping cart solutions will include connections to payments authorization and capture services. Or, you may have your IT resources program payments transactions interfaces. Whatever you chose, be sure you understand the up-front and ongoing payments costs.

Bundled solutions seem simpler when you are choosing payments processing, but may lock you into relatively more expense on every transaction from that point on. Easy implementation may be attractive during startup, but as you grow you may find unbundled and transparent processing allows you to measure and manage payments to reduce your costs and improve your profits.

Another important factor will be the extent and the type of payments fraud your website business might attract. For example, if your website sells digital content you may have to positively verify customer identity well before your shopping cart process concludes.

After a payment is authorized and you deliver content through a download, if that payment is later charged back because the card number was stolen you have little recourse to recover the payment, nor your content.

eCommerce digital content sales are currently the frontier, the wild west of payments fraud. Expect a continuing arms race between the good guys and the bad guys, and on-going fraud prevention innovations.

Importantly, if your chargebacks exceed 1% over a period of time, you may be assessed penalties, and have significant reserves held back our of your sales revenue and not deposited in your checking account until after a significant delay. You may even be denied the ability to process card payments.

PayPal

Experts estimate 15% of U.S. eCommerce transactions in 2008 went through PayPal, not counting eBay transactions. So, for those readers who are today or planning to be eCommerce enterprises here is a PayPal overview from the **PAYMENTS POWER** perspective.

First some history. PayPal is only a little over a decade old, but their growth and change has been fast and dramatic.

The reason many individuals went to PayPal when it was originally offered was the fear of hackers seeing and stealing their credit card numbers online. PayPal cut its card processing teeth on higher risk payments, so they have developed a core competence in eCommerce risk.

PayPal was aimed at individuals, what is labeled P2P, and facilitated the incredible growth of eBay, and is now part of that company.

Today PayPal offers several levels of eCommerce payment processing, for both *In$* and *Out$*. PayPal accounts and balances have been described as a new type of money. And, although PayPal representatives are careful to say their focus remains on eCommerce, I believe their strategy will move PayPal into mainstream brick and mortar commerce too. Let's see why.

First PayPal Developer's Conference, November 3-4, 2009

Mid-year 2009 PayPal began opening their payments offerings programming interfaces to outside developers. This move was built on previous success in the parent company's eBay Developers Program.

Outside beta developers demonstrated applications with PayPal capabilities integrated at PayPal's first developers' conference in San Francisco. They provided a website to access APIs and SDKs for what PayPal calls their newer architecture, Adaptive Payments. (API is Application Programming Interface, and SDK is Software Development Kit).

Enterprise Services

In addition, the company has opened channels for reselling PayPal eCommerce and merchant services, gateway and virtual terminal solutions. Payments orchestrators will be able to configure and facilitate your addition of these payments capabilities, as bundled and unbundled solutions.

Many of their stated goals are in harmony with **PAYMENTS POWER**, even if their approach differs somewhat. For example, their answer to frustration with the traditional credit card processing of qualified, mid and non-qualified is to offer a very simple bundled pricing model that varies only by volume, not by card association interchange classification. Currently this can work partly because they deal only with Card Not Present transactions. However, there appears to be a significant payments cost premium paid for that simplicity.

Risk and Underwriting

PayPal reports an overall fraud loss of only 0.25%. Skeptics wonder how they calculate that performance, but acknowledge that they have the history and the risk data.

One of the exhibitors at the PayPal Developers Conference told me a story of helping hundreds of new private medical practices. The doctors had all been rejected by other merchant service underwriters as too risky, but with his 'Pay Your Medical Bill Online' application, all the accounts were accepted for PayPal merchant services.

I interviewed a long time eBay seller who felt that without PayPal his home business could never have been possible. While he related that the combination of eBay charges and PayPal costs have increased over the years, on balance he is satisfied, even pleased.

Rewards Research and Capability

Redeeming rewards points has become less satisfying. There are many reasons, and PayPal referenced research that shows people want something different today from traditional rewards programs. Most of us would like to redeem our rewards point or frequent flyer miles for everyday items instead of big expensive events like a long trip. Because of this shift in attitudes PayPal has developed the interesting capability to redeem points for PayPal money that can be immediately spent anywhere online.

While there is much discussion about the overhead cost of compliance requirements for rewards programs with monetary value, (the Patriot Act, etc.) their focus on payments rewards topics clearly reflects a PayPal innovation strategy.

Payments Chain with PayPal

The following payments chain diagram includes well-known PayPal elements. Note the Seller's PayPal account in the diagram upper right green box. This can be an enterprise account, somewhat like a financial institution business checking account. It facilitates eCommerce through PayPal payments.

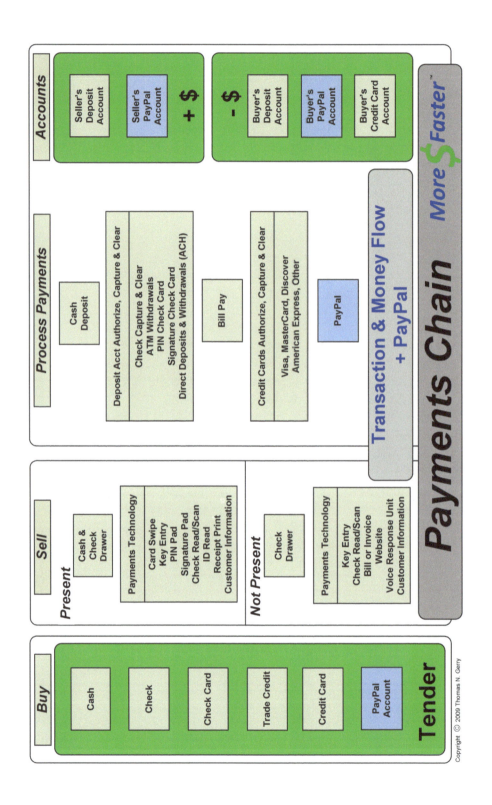

The biggest drawback is the funds are only usable instantly for on-line transactions. Upon request PayPal will transfer funds from this account to the seller's traditional financial institution deposit account at no cost with a direct ACH deposit, reportedly with only a few days delay.

PayPal representatives at the conference were encouraging balance accumulation and retention with competitive Money Market interest rates. Is this an opening salvo in a national battle with traditional financial institutions for business deposit balances? Or has PayPal become just another kind of financial institution?

Today there are many ways to put the eCommerce puzzle together. You may wish to understand more deeply the potential combinations for your business model to maximize customer sales, minimize payments costs, and keep more profit. If you are interested, keep reading. A more complex diagram may be for you.

Behind the Curtain – With PayPal

The true extent of PayPal capabilities are better understood with a more complex *Behind the curtain* payments chain diagram. In the upper left corner notice the PayPal capability associated with Bill Pay.

Just as an individual buyer can save time and money paying a utility bill online, soon they will be able to use their bill pay systems to send money to individuals by entering an e-mail address or cell phone number. Neither the sender nor the receiver has to have a PayPal account initially, but the payment e-mail/cell phone notification to the receiver will make it fast and easy to open a PayPal account and use the funds received.

For online shopping the funds received are usable right away, but if the receiving person wants to use the funds with their traditional bank account, as previously mentioned, then PayPal provides a free ACH transfer.

Near the bottom of the left hand side of the diagram you will see that PayPal offers ways to pay suppliers, affiliates or agents. This can be done with spreadsheet uploads or through programming integration with an accounts payable application. More detail on this later in the **Out$** portion of this chapter.

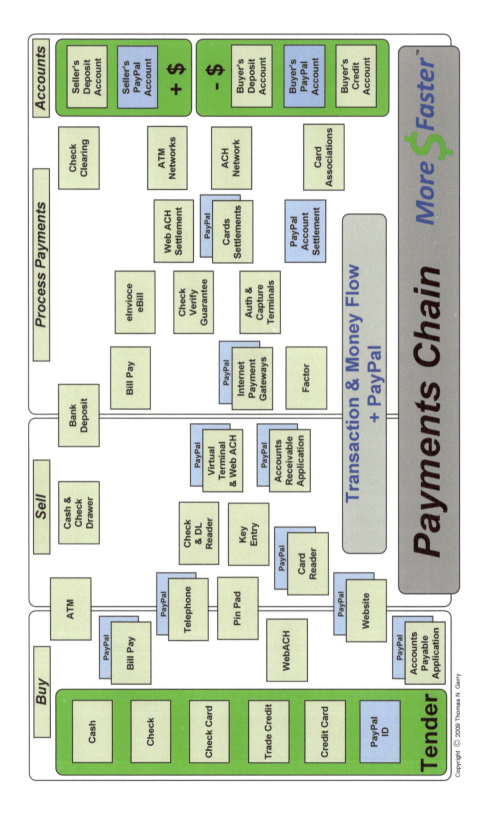

As you scan this diagram, you will see PayPal has much to offer for all types of buyers and sellers including enterprise PayPal accounts. Let's explore these capabilities with a **PAYMENTS POWER** perspective.

In$

For **In$** there are at least five options; three for those without existing merchant credit card processing and two for those that already have a merchant payments relationship. One does not even require a website, just an e-mail address. For those that are website based there are various shopping cart options available. There are HTML and API types of website integration for different levels of technical sophistication, and customer privacy protection.

In addition to **In$** integrated to websites, PayPal also offers a Virtual Terminal for payments received by telephone, fax or mail. This is a web-based service that is easy to use in the back office, a CNP, *Card not present*, situation. Is this eCommerce or *Brick and Mortar*?

Costs disclosed on the PayPal site are generally 1.9% to 2.9% plus 30 cents per transaction. In some options the Virtual Terminal capability is included. In others there is a $30 monthly charge. (Prices are subject to change, of course).

Out$

For **Out$** PayPal offers two electronic approaches to replace paper check payments. This service handles other currencies in addition to U.S. dollars. More on this in the next chapter about cross border payments.

MassPay

You can upload simple files to make payments electronically. Multiple currencies are handled with individual files per currency type. There is a maximum individual transaction amount of $10,000 US dollars. The fee disclosed on the PayPal website is 2% of the transaction amount, with a $1 dollar maximum. If the payer converts currency there is a 2.5% exchange fee as well.

Pay API

You can also integrate electronic **Out$** with their Pay API. This alternative supports single transaction responses. For example, a bank website might support the exchange of rewards points for a PayPal deposit, real money that can be used instantly for eCommerce shopping. With the Pay API, notice can be communicated right away to the waiting customer that the reward points have been exchanged for PayPal money.

Payment notification e-mail includes a link for receiving these payments. Naturally, if a recipient does not already have one, a free PayPal account is offered to use the money.

In a way PayPal is a trusted escrow agent that enables strangers to send goods before having usable funds, and to pay for goods before gaining physical possession.

PayPal Crystal Ball

eCommerce Applications

We have seen attempts to compete with PayPal that have not succeeded in any significant way as yet. In eCommerce you will want to keep scanning for payments methods that can bring either more customer choices or lower payments costs, hopefully both.

If you have not looked at eCheck capabilities, you should. eCheck can be implemented today with web-based ACH. You can use either an independent or a bundled version of eCheck integrated in your current checkout technology – just be sure you know what it costs you as a portion of your sales dollar. eCheck may be your least costly payments method compared to a card not present transaction.

Mobile Applications

Cell phone innovation is following a familiar path as the technology shrinks in cost and size while the power and bandwidth grows and expands. Just as the PC went from a toy for nerds to a ubiquitous tool for individuals of all ages and interests, and a mainstream enterprise and network technology; so too is the mobile phone world following that path. Check out the device an iPhone slips into that includes a card swipe and wireless payments processing – just search for PAYware Mobile.

Today there are applications emerging built on combinations of cell phone built-in sensors (GPS, compass and others) and massive network databases that truly expand personal and business productivity. Mobile payments integration alternatives are competing for acceptance among early adopters. You may want to think ahead about additional customer convenience, additional revenue and another type of payments costs to measure and manage in the **PAYMENTS POWER** framework.

In 2011 the ACH code for internet payments, WEB, is being expanded to cover mobile payments applications. Picture this, your system sends a text offer, your customer responds with a 'yes', and a checking account electronic payment is created. Recent studies reveal that many people prefer text over actually talking on their cell phones.

What if, in planning her busy day, your customer could enter a purchase and payment on her mobile phone before stopping at your store to quickly pick up something? Your staff could get it off the shelf and package and receipt the item during a slack moment before she arrives. Could that be an advantage for you to offer her before your competitors do? Only experimentation will tell.

Brick and Mortar Solutions

While the PayPal Gateway currently lacks support for PIN-based check card transactions, they do support card present transactions with a PC attached card swipe reader. They have much experience with eCheck in the eCommerce world, and they may also add all that to their virtual terminal offerings someday.

Credit Accounts for Buyers – The flip side

What Payments Chain player ends up with the interchange payoff? Interchange is funded out of the seller's revenue, and is deposited into the credit or debit account issuer. That would be the buyer's bank, the issuing credit card company, or AMEX.

Large volume retailers have issued cards to buyers through negotiated bank alliances. They earn at least a portion of the interchange back.

Now you can get a PayPal Extras MasterCard, eBay MasterCard or perhaps a line of credit called PayPal Smart Connect (which has no Visa, nor MasterCard branding). What PayPal is doing though is different than a retail store card. This is something new.

Wow! Just think about the kind of information from online buyers that flows through the PayPal chain. For example, wouldn't this be a great source of prospects for branded credit cards?

And why not avoid the card association fees as well as capture all the interchange paid by sellers by becoming a credit line lender with Smart Connect, at least for low risk buyers?

Bankers should be watching these PayPal developments with interest. Other payments innovations are coming from the internet world. Outside the eBay space where PayPal has an almost impregnable position, competitors are emerging.

Internet "Crystal Ball"

One of the technology thought leaders, Tim O'Reilly, who coined the term Web 2.0, has voiced a caution about any one of the giants becoming the only choice on the internet. Apple, Microsoft, Google, even PayPal are all naturally competing for dominant positions, but the world is best served by a rich and varied competition, not an outright win by any one approach or mindset.

Heck, if that happened we would just have another indifferent bureaucracy to deal with. Big winners almost always become complacent and inner directed without competition.

This holds true in the payments industry. The most frustrating payments statements come from some of the biggest players.

Internet eCommerce payments are still fragmented, even with PayPal in the lead. There will be many exciting innovations in coming years, even as the edges blur and there is cross-over back to brick and mortar.

Take Action

1. Decide if you will increase sales with a business Pay-Pal account.

2. Start a separate PayPal *M$* and *F$* measurement

3. "PayPal is now Open" – Look for innovations from outside developers that integrate PayPal capabilities.

4. Compare costs from independent resellers that offer solutions including PayPal services and payments.

5. For *In$* check out the PC Gateway and Virtual Terminal, with or without PayPal settlement services, but PayPal does not yet support PIN nor eChecks (as of end of 2009).

6. For *Out$* consider PayPal's MassPay – Simple and low tech, low cost, or Pay API, more flexible, but standard merchant service pricing, handling 24 currencies and 65 countries (end of 2009).

More$Faster

www.paymentspower.com

13 INCREASE CROSS BORDER PAYMENTS PROFITS

If you receive or pay across borders, you may be incurring significant additional payments costs that reduce your profits. This chapter is a brief introduction to encourage you to analyze innovations that are just becoming more widely used alternatives to legacy payments methods.

Three payments types are reviewed:

1. Credit Cards

2. Cross Border ACH

3. PayPal

13 INCREASE CROSS BORDER PAYMENTS PROFITS

If your business receives money from customers or pays money to suppliers across national boundaries, you may have substantial payments costs, fees, delays and risks.

In addition, OFAC, the Office of Foreign Assets Control of the U.S. Treasury, requires information about cross border payments to ensure no terrorist or criminal activities are supported with these transactions.

Credit Cards

For consumers credit cards have made purchasing easy in most countries around the world. On several overseas business trips I checked the card statement foreign exchange rates against the rates I got at local banks and money exchange offices. Almost always the credit card exchange rate was better.

As a seller, though, you experience higher interchange rates from non US issued credit cards. You may want to assess the importance of this higher cost and consider alternatives such as cross-border ACH transactions.

Cross Border ACH

There are reports some companies suffer currency exchange cost up to 6% of the transaction amount, plus $15 to $25 dollars per cross border payment. Even if the supplier you pay has a local US dollar denominated account, if you can save that trading partner some payments costs, you may benefit in negotiating purchases.

For *In$*, there are also the effects of varying customer preferences in different countries to be considered. In Germany, for example, there are a much higher proportion of electronic payments direct from deposit accounts than credit card payments. So, if your Internet checkout does not include this direct payment withdrawn from a demand deposit bank account, you may not be making all the sales you could to German buyers.

For **Out$,** the withdrawals to fund the payments occur same day, but the supplier may get the money up to seven days later or longer. The Mass Payment service from PayPal handles up to 18 different currencies as of the end of 2009, including the US Dollar, in the following list:

Cross Border Money

US Dollar	Mexican Peso
Australian Dollar	New Zealand Dollar
Canadian Dollar	Norwegian Krone
Czech Koruna	Polish Zloty
Danish Krone	Pound Sterling
Euro	Singapore Dollar
Hong Kong Dollar	Swedish Krona
Hungarian Forint	Swiss Franc
Israeli New Shekel	Yen

26

Although I expect this list to grow, it may be hard to find a cost effective electronic payment processor for some import/export business opportunities.

So, for cross border payments you will want to discover, measure and track foreign exchange fees and all transaction costs and delays in completing payments.

There may be substantial profit improvements and cash flow benefits from payments innovations available today or emerging soon.

Take Action

1. Identify and measure additional **In$** costs – compare to checks, international wires and international trade credit practices:

   - Interchange cost of Non US Credit Cards

   - Currency exchange fees

   - Additional bank processing fees

2. Cross Border ACH is evolving, but is promising for some business situations.

3. Check out web-based Cross Border ACH origination which is just becoming available for **Out$.**

4. PayPal MassPay is available today for Cross Border **Out$** payments – use payment chains, **L$** and **F$** to see if it fits your needs.

5. Establish a scan for Cross Border development in the eCommerce world to lower future payments costs.

14 CONTINUOUSLY IMPROVE PAYMENTS

The **PAYMENTS POWER** approach is a knowledge-based decision making framework to help uncover profits hidden in your payments systems, and strengthen your competitive advantage. The **PAYMENTS POWER** framework is comprehensive:

1. All types of payments in, **In$,** and payments out, **Out$.**

2. Payment Chains to visualize current and future flows

3. Simple measures let you easily compare costs and speed

4. Improve, Switch and Add strategies

Three Stages of Continuous Improvement are suggested so you can act quickly and yet improve profit every year:

1. Best Processing-Transparency & Measurement

2. Team Education, Motivation & Action

3. Customers and Suppliers Experiments

M$** and **F$ can be used at an enterprise level and by payment type for your business units to measure the results of training and experiments, to spot positive or negative trends with visual displays, to benchmark performance store to store, or business unit to business unit.

Beyond this book, resources are available through the website and e-mail to help you implement and continuously improve profits. www.paymentspower.com

14 CONTINUOUSLY IMPROVE PAYMENTS

Knowledge-Based Competitive Advantage

In a recent book, *Competition Demystified*, Bruce Greenwald and Judd Kahn laid out in simple terms the three classic sustainable competitive advantages – scale, intellectual property and customer captivity. In addition, they talked about a wild card in the last chapter of their book.

Here is why. They found very few companies have achieved and maintained any of the three classic positions, but in all industries there are significant and long lasting variations in performance of individual enterprises. How do the best performers achieve this without one of the three classic competitive strategies?

The wild card is this combination - **Customer focus, knowledge-based superior execution, cost control and tightly managed cash flow**.

PAYMENTS POWER was created to help you play this wild card. Any company of any size can use payments insights to increase customer focus, knowledge-based superior execution, cost control and cash flow without much capital investment, and improve profits quickly.

When you finish this chapter you will have reviewed all the practical **PAYMENTS POWER** tools created to give you the competitive advantages listed in the previous paragraph. I sincerely hope you will improve your profits substantially. Here are the tools:

1. The measurement framework that includes all the possible types of payments, *In$* and *Out$*.

2. The payments metric innovations of *M$, L$* and *F$* to assess, compare and track payment performance, and your efforts to improve your profits and cash flow.

3. Payments Chains to visualize the processes.

4. The three strategies of Improve, Switch or Add.

5. The three Continuous Improvement Stages.

Comprehensive Framework – Knowledge to Action

The worksheets, the step by step approach, the common sense measures, the process diagrams I call Payments Chains, the staged implementation of the three strategies have been forged in the field testing of **PAYMENTS POWER**. Many types and sizes of enterprises have provided reality checks for the approach.

Do the **PAYMENTS POWER** tools, work? Yes. Can they be improved? You bet! This is like a treasure hunt, with you finding your own profits. I am continuing to discover new pockets of opportunity. I look forward to sharing your stories in a future edition.

PAYMENTS POWER defines two simple kinds of payments measures that are easily displayed visually, *M$* and *L$* for *How Much*, and *F$*, for *How Fast*. For sales the metrics are *M$* and *F$.* For disbursements we use *L$* and *F$.*

M$F Stages	
1 **Best Processing**	• Transparency • Measurement • Self-sufficiency • Lower Processing costs
2 **Team**	• Policy changes • Education • Motivation • Lower Interchange costs
3 **Customers and Suppliers**	• Experiments • Loyalty • Rewards • Benchmarking • Revenue and all costs

Action Stages

You can gain more and more profit by building on changes and re-setting priorities as the measurements improve. These stages are somewhat sequential.

Stage 1 – Best Processing is relatively fast and easy and the transparency realized is needed to effectively perform stages 2 and 3.

Stage 2 – Team changes should be faster and easier when you have simple payments measures to show the effect of training, experiments and policy changes.

Stage 3 - Customers & Suppliers, experiments can be started once you have the fact-based management, and additional payments choices Stage 1 may indicate.

Stage 3 - An important additional insight

Rewards and Loyalty are relationship tactics. Understand your repeat customers' and suppliers' payments behaviors and preferences to harvest a significant portion of your potential profit improvement. Neither merchant processing statements nor bank account statements can reveal those patterns over time.

Here are the steps that will let you identify these keys and give you some ideas on experiments to change those that matter:

1. Produce three months of customer payments history reports and file exports.

2. Sort by customer or if you do not have specific individual customer data, sort by customer type or segment.

3. Look for repeating or disparate patterns – does a customer always use the same payment type, or is there a mix, for example, sometimes PIN debit, sometimes a check, and sometimes a frequent flyer rewards credit card?
Look for returns, adjustments and payments reversals patterns too.

4. Sum up amounts over the 3 months for each payment type and match up the payment type costs you previously developed with the **PAYMENTS POWER** framework and worksheets.

5. Experiment to change your customers' payments behaviors on the largest and most costly payment types.

6. Change your polices, practices and training as needed.

7. Measure experiment results and adjust as needed, and continually repeat these steps.

In the **EXTRAS** appendix is a summary level action plan template that you can adapt or copy for project management of the stages.

Of course, for your action plans you may want more detail task breakdowns and responsibility assignments. Do not get too detailed, but do use project management best practices to avoid stalling out and losing momentum. For example, I recommend very aggressive individual task durations with an overall project buffer to manage uncertainties. The other key is to let your project people focus - do not try to make them multi-task, or you will likely experience unacceptable schedule slippages.

Payments Power Results – Visual Displays

After **Stage 1** you will have measurements you can use for trend spotting, store to store comparisons, and analysis drill down. Because **M$,** and **L$** are simple to understand profit measures and **F$** is just a common sense cash flow measure, your team members and your decision makers should quickly gain a payments performance awareness and perspective.

These measures are ideal for visual displays so everyone can see changes, improvements month to month, quarter to quarter and year over year. Here is an **In$** example showing cost improvements and the effect on **M$** month by month.

This visual display shows three months progress in several payments types. Although this example highlights **M$** you should consider displaying your **F$** cash flow speed improvement too.

Payments Improvement
Credit Cards, Checks Cards & Checks

M$	July $ 96.11	Aug $ 96.98	Sept $ 97.11
	Costs	Costs	Costs
AMEX	4.2%	3.2%	3.2%
Visa, MC, Disc	3.2%	3.4%	2.3 %
Signature Debit	2.3%	2.3%	1.7%
PIN Debit	1.1%	1.2%	1.1%
Electronic Check	1.6%	1.9%	1.6%
Paper Check	1.6%	0.0%	0.0%

PAYMENTS
POWER

Make your visual displays easy to update and easy to read so your team members can see the profit improvements they are making. Avoid too much detail, and change your displays as you experiment to spotlight what you are trying to improve.

Benchmarking – How do you compare?

The statistics available on payments in the US are impressive, but not too useful for enterprise decision makers.

When I asked one of the world payments experts where to find good information for cash, currency and coin, he advised me, "The simple answer is that there are no reliable statistics on either the value or the number of cash transactions in the US. Some estimates, however, do exist." David Humphrey has years of US and international experience. He revealed that some models give a reasonable measure of issued currency stock, but no good method really reports the flow or velocity of currency and coin.

Even the NACHA statistics have only recently been brought more in alignment with Federal Reserve payments study's methodology. Neither NACHA nor the FED give us an easy comparison to benchmark our own payments data and trends. By the time the FED studies are published they are old news.

Here is an idea:

A NATIONAL PAYMENTS POWER BENCHMARKING DATABASE.

Profit and Cash Flow Improvement Benchmarking

If you find the **PAYMENTS POWER** framework and payments performance indicators valuable, you may want to consider joining in a unique quarterly national benchmarking study.

The objective is to give back to the participants market comparisons to what their enterprises are experiencing and achieving individually. Go to the website if you would like to learn more about this benchmarking study. www.paymentspower.com

What do you think?

Is **PAYMENTS POWER** valuable to you? Let me know. E-mail me at tomgerry@paymentspower.com .

Check out the **EXTRAS** section following this chapter for some of the resources that are available on the website.

Take Action

Establish three aims:

1. **Profit** – savings in payments processing

2. **Risk** – compliance with payments privacy requirements and manage payments losses

3. **Control** – transparency and knowledge directed action – Better Decisions, Superior Execution

Act - Prioritize and stage improvements:

1. Make payments processing transparent and measurable – use Visual Displays

2. Engage your team to improve profits with process and procedure

3. Experiment with customer and supplier experiences, measure improvements and repeat continuously.

Benchmark your payments systems performance.

Share your stories.

Extras

1. **PAYMENTS POWER** Profit Improvement Estimator

2. Summary Action Plan

3. Website Resources

    a. Blog

    a. Team Presentations

    b. Assessment Spreadsheets

    c. Visual Displays

    d. White Papers

Payments Power
Profit Improvement

Current Situation		
Net Profit as % of Sales		5.0%
Money In		
Payments Costs as a % of Sales		3.00%
Usable $ Added to Bank Balance of each $100 of Sales	*M$	$97.00
Money Out		
Payments Costs as a % of Disbursements		2.00%
Total $ Reduced in Bank Balance to Pay each $100 Out	*L$	$102.00
Total Payments Costs as % of Sales		**4.8%**
More$Faster Improvement		
Reduction in Payments In Costs - basis points		60
Reduction in Payments Out Costs - basis points		50
Money In		
Payments Costs as a % of Sales		2.40%
Usable $ Added to Bank Balance of each $100 of Sales	*M$	$97.60
Money Out		
Payments Costs as a % of Disbursements		1.50%
Total $ Reduced in Bank Balance to Pay each $100 Out	*L$	$101.50
Total Payments Costs as a % of Sales		**3.8%**
Profit Up from 5% to 6%, an increase of 20%		

* M$ and L$ are the Payments Power performance measures for all types of Money In and Money Out.

Summary Action Plan

PAYMENTS POWER

More $ Faster

Summary Action Plan

Tasks	Who	When	Status
I. Assess, Plan and Prepare			
Assess current payments - 3 months & agreements			
Decide what to change and modify Action Plan			
Gather information and documents			
Make applications to underwriting			
Order terminals, components, and signage			
II. Act - Implement and Train			
Set-up terminals and components			
Train			
Test			
Establish user IDs and passwords			
Try 1st and 2nd levels of support			
Post customer communications & disclosures			
Reconcile and audit			
III. Process, Measure and Continually Improve			
Set-up visual controls			
Post baseline metrics			
Analyze and post monthly performance			
Develop and implement improvements			
Celebrate success			
IV. Repeat for Stage 2 and Stage 3			

1

Website Resources - www.paymentspower.com

Team Presentations

Various educational and training presentation slides and notes are offered on the website.

They include:

- US National Payments Trends Analysis

- Assessment Tools

- Action Tactics

- Results Measurement and Visual Displays

Assessment Spreadsheets

A set of analysis templates are available on the website.

They include all types of tender, for payments in and payments out:

- Currency and Coin

- Checks

- Trade Credit

- Cards

- ePayments

ACKNOWLEDGEMENTS

John Gerry, Harlin Financial Services, who opened the curtain on the wizard of OZ—the strange, fragmented, complex payments systems world.

Business leaders who shared their stories with me. John Hutchison, Cary Kresge, Scott Green, Robert Vaughn, Maggie Howe, Mary Kenney, Phillip Pritchett, Andy Fass, Debbie Sheehan, Adam Gerry, Steve Little and Al Davidson. Kevin and Lee Acker of Re/Max 200 and Fred Thompson, with Lynn Cunningham's diligent research.

Randy Phelps, Sid Fingerhut and their powerful growth team.

Business associates and friends who gave me critical thoughts and suggestions on drafts. Mike Milvain and Wayne LeRoux, Corbin Shaver, Ed Ginn, Cindy Pyburn, Joyce Dye, Phil Snyder, Mel Ora, Harry Johnson, and George Bassous. Lawrence (Mitch) Mitchell, our friend who showed me the payments in and out perspective of an eBay seller.

Dan Fisher, author, consultant and former FED regional board member, Copper River Group. Tim Clifford, entrepreneur and lockbox expert, TMR Associates. Roger Bishop and Phil Haumiller. Jeff Fortney. John Hayes, author and creator or Peachtree software and FTrans.

Raj Shivdasani, Scott Hansen and Sam Kilmer.

Value makers field testing PAYMENTS POWER. Ron Fraser and Tom Bradberry.

Advisors on targeting a business book to produce value. Dick Hissam, James Halloran and Dan Fisher.

Money and payments system expert. Dr. David B. Humphrey. FSU.

Agents, writing experts and editors. Barbara Odum and Renate Gaisser. Elizabeth Marshall & Janet Goldstein. Cheryl Shea volunteered the final conceptual edit and did a magnificent job with this challenge.

NOTES AND REFERENCES

Selected Payments Links:

Visa Interchange
usa.visa.com/merchants/operations/interchange_rates.html

MasterCard Interchange
www.mastercard.com/us/merchant/support/interchange_rates.html

NACHA
www.nacha.org

Other payments associations, processors, gateways and clearing houses can be found with online searches.

Payments Studies:

The 2010 Federal Reserve Payments Study, Noncash Payment Trends in the United States 2006-2009, Release December 8, 2010, Federal Reserve System.

Debit Card Interchange Fees and Routing, Notice of proposed rulemaking, December, 2010, Federal Reserve System.

The Electronic Payments Study, A Survey of Electronic Payments for the 2007 Federal Reserve Payments Study, Research sponsored by the Federal Reserve System Performed by Dove Consulting, a Division of Hitachi Consulting, Released March 2008, Federal Reserve System.

The Check Sample Study, A Survey of Depository Institutions for the 2007 Federal Reserve Payments Study, Research sponsored by the Federal Reserve System Performed by Global Concepts, Released March 2008, Federal Reserve System.

The Depository Institutions Payments Study, A Survey of Depository Institutions for the 2007 Federal Reserve Payments Study, Global Concepts Research sponsored by the Federal Reserve System, Released March 2008.

Year End 2008. NACHA PowerPoint statistics presentation.

Replacement of cash by cards in US consumer payments, David B. Humphrey, Journal of Economics & Business 2004.

World of Choice: Consumer Payment Preferences. Daniel Hough, Mark Riddle, Chris Allen and Melissa Fox, BAI Banking Strategies, January February 2009.

Payments Books & Sources:

Digital Transactions, Trends in the Electronic Exchange of Value. John Stewart, Editor in Chief, Borland Hill Media, LLC, Published monthly.

Insiders Guide to ePayment Management, 30 Tactics Leading Merchants Use to Capture Hidden Profits, CyberSource, 2008.

Selling Online 2.0, Migrating from eBay to Amazon, craigslist, and your own E-Commerce Website. Michael Miller, QUE 2009.

The Merchant's Guide. Michael E. Shatz, The Merchant's Guide, LLC, eBook published and updated for several years.

Use the Credit Crisis to Grow Your B2B Business, A Proven Strategy for Enduring Competitive Advantage and Business Growth, John B. Hayes, Plain Talk Press, 2008.

Strategy & Measurement Books & Sources:

Competition Demystified, A Radically Simplified Approach to Business Strategy, Bruce Greenwald, Judd Kahn, Portfolio –the Penguin Group, 2005.

Competing on Analytics, The New Science of Winning. Thomas H. Davenport, Jeanne G. Harris, Harvard Business School Press, 2007.

ABOUT THE AUTHOR

Tom Gerry has 39 years' experience in business and the payments world as a proven team leader, salesperson, consultant, entrepreneur, speaker and author. He has broad experience in marketing, sales, implementations and training, project management and application development of shrink wrapped and semi-custom software.

He started learning about payments early in his career at an innovative regional bank which offered their own branded credit card long before Visa and MasterCard gained national acceptance. That bank deployed online ATMs, some of the original devices, in the early 70's.

Tom gained insight from his work in technology development and process re-engineering in many stages and facets of the decades long transition from paper to electronic payments.

He was working with a group of patriots and banking entrepreneurs in the parliament building in Estonia when they took the historic vote proclaiming their independence from the Soviet Union in 1991. His work contributed, in a small part, to their establishment of a privately capitalized banking industry with advanced technology payments systems replacing the completely ineffective central government run banks, and the worthless Soviet currency.

Tom founded three consulting and technology companies—one reached $20 million in sales in 2008. He has leadership skills in setting strategic direction and creating winning competitive campaigns—one company achieved #1 national ranking.

At Harland Financial Solutions Tom lead a team that designed, developed and launched a national deposit performance benchmarking analysis and measurement service in just nine months. His cross functional group was recognized with a Harland Pillar Award nomination for Competitive Advantage. Harland is known as a national leader in payments.

In addition to this book, Tom has authored many white papers, been quoted in industry publications, created and delivered seminars and a webinar series, and made speeches at national and regional conventions.

www.ingramcontent.com/pod-product-compliance
Lightning Source LLC
Chambersburg PA
CBHW041417050326

40689CB00002B/543